MOVEMENT AWARENESS AND

MOVEMENT AWARENESS and CREATIVITY

Leah Bartal
Nira Ne'eman

DANCE
BOOKS

First published in 1975

This edition published in 2001 by Dance Books Ltd
4 Lenten Street, Alton, Hampshire GU34 1HG

Printed in Great Britain by H. Charlesworth & Co., Huddersfield

ISBN 1 85273 084 6

Dedicated to Nira's patient and participating family and to Alon

Foreword

I believe that this book will make a most valuable contribution to the teaching of dance and drama in this country, and also to the understanding of movement in general. For many years educational movement and modern dance have been dominated by the work of Rudolf Laban, to the exclusion of almost any other approach. But recently, many teachers and Colleges of Education lecturers, without rejecting Laban's theories, have begun to consider it necessary to try out other styles and approaches. While in the world of professional dance, though it is still dominated by the ballet, by Graham and jazz, choreographers have begun to use a variety of styles and to see the possibility of integrating different techniques in various ways.

All these developments, both in education and in the professional dance world, can only be based on a real understanding of the structure and potentialities of the human body, both physically and expressively – for the relationship between mind and body is absolute.

This book transcends styles and schools and goes back to basic principles. And its virtues spring from a fundamental understanding of the nature of movement and all its possible complexities.

First of all I would like to commend its breadth of approach. The authors discuss the body as an instrument that can be 'educated' in a great variety of ways, and I use the word 'education' to make a sharp distinction from 'training'. This idea leads me on to the second virtue of the book, for training is a very limited concept, while education suggests that the body is a highly expressive instrument, in many respects more expressive than the voice. I believe that even if one is working in a manner that might be called functional, loosening the spine or strengthening a limb, a quality of concentration or mental involvement is essential if the exercise is to have any value. And the real expressive qualities of the body emerge from this. The authors suggest a great number of ways in which this unity of mind and body can be realised and developed.

It remains only for the enterprising teacher to discover for himself or herself the riches that lie in the following pages.

John Allen
Principal, Central School of Speech
and Drama, London

Contents

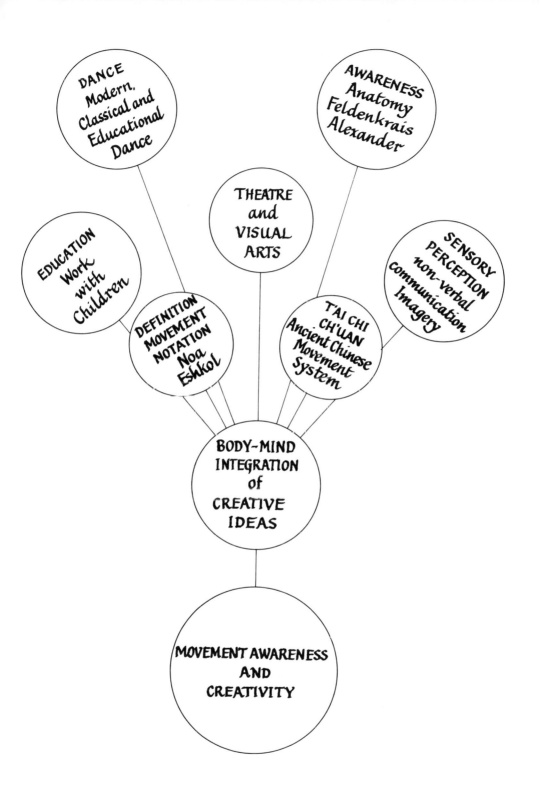

1 Where we begin

Much did I learn from my tutors,
more from my friends,
and most from my students.

Rabbi Akiba

Our approach to movement is directed not only at teachers of movement and drama, though this book is mainly intended for them; but at anybody interested in developing clear and meaningful ways of using the body, and in increasing human perceptiveness through the development of imagination and creativity.

The book starts with a short scientific introduction; proceeds through various ways of working, including awareness of the body, sensory perception, use of imagination; to a set of structured lessons, work with children, and an experimental three-year course planned for a drama school.

We have both worked for many years using different methods, and our present way of working involves a synthesis of elements from them all, from East and West, which we have found valuable to the deeper understanding of movement, and of the body-mind relationship in general.

'After three years of training as a dance teacher,' Lea once told an interviewer, 'and thinking I knew everything about movement there was to know – irrespective of the fact that my shoulders were as high and tight as on the day I entered school, and I was still not able to go into a "deep *plié*" in second position – something had to be done. . . . I started working with Noa Eshkol at the Chamber Theatre in Tel-Aviv.'

And Nira added, 'All through my studying movement and dance in education I was looking for a possibility of thinking and imagining movement. In meeting Dr Feldenkrais I was fascinated by the scientific and logically clear approach to movement, by the infinite possibility of varying movements with one part of the body, such as the pelvis or the shoulder, alone.'

What we have evolved, separately and together, is a method on the one hand of helping our students make their bodies the disciplined, well-tuned instruments necessary for any creative activity; and on the other of developing their artistic perceptions, to make them aware that all art has shape. We try to find each person's creative potential, and expand it to the utmost. Thus we work on defined movement compositions by students on their own, finding in these the indications of how much has been absorbed, how far the student is able to express himself. For actors particularly these experiences become an infinite resource on which to draw in the creation of mood and character.

We use improvisation, leading to composition, to open the way for the spontaneous expression of the individual, which is an integral part of every artistic creation, as important as the sketch to the painter, the model to the sculptor, the musical improvisation to the composer. For the good actor, improvisation is the source of self-revelation and expression – what Constantin Stanislavski called the 'Inner Creative State'. It is important to anyone using movement as a way of expressing himself, dancer or actor, but also important for everyone wanting to lead a full life.

The body as an instrument is capable of creating its own language. As an educated person has learned to express himself freely, so the well-tuned body can sing a song, tell a story or assume the refined shape of a sculpture. Linguistic concepts are based on precise structures so that letters and words make it possible to shape sentences, stories and poems. The movements of the fully aware body can be organised to be as expressive as any language.

An individual acts according to an image he has of himself. Many people do it without being aware of this image. If, however, one wants to develop the whole potential of the person, this image has to be an integration between senses and awareness based on scientific investigation. A whole person will combine awareness and sensitivity to express himself with joy, freedom and feeling thus this communication with the outside world.

As water can change its density, so the human body in movement can be changeable: it can be soft, slow and weak, or it can hasten its flow, becoming gradually stronger, faster and more vigorous until it is like a stormy sea with huge waves flooding the shore; it can also become rigid like ice or turn into vapour or even pure spirit.

An alive person can allow his energy to flow freely and thus fully express himself.

In our work the human body has to be able to perform an enormous variety of functions. Any person engaged in daily activities – if he is using his potential fully – may become a highly sensitive instrument, performing physical tasks, expressing feelings and reacting to outside stimulus. And the actor, who may be called on to represent any human experience, has to be exceptionally perceptive and sensitive, for he has to communicate his experience to an audience through his expressive abilities. His personal interpretation is needed to bring to life the character created by the author.

Our intention is to show ways of working with the body that will enable the individual to become aware of the tensions governing his behaviour. Everyone's private world is dramatised in his body. To master this highly complex instrument one has to know what one is doing, what amount of tension is needed for any action at any given time and what amount of tension is superfluous.

We are trying to discover the healthy organic principles common to all human beings, We want to understand the body-mind relationship underlying human behaviour, and the basic expressive impulses inherent in humans and animals. The nearer a person is to his own instincts, the more aware of his own archetypal roots, the better will he be able to turn himself into a free-flowing instrument in touch with the inner nature he has in common with all other human beings.

Musicians have instruments other than themselves, sculptors and painters have materials. The rest of us, including actors, dancers and singers *are* themselves the instrument. Therefore human beings have to undergo a process that can be compared to the tuning of an instru-

5

ment – balancing the energies flowing in the body, balancing the psycho-physical tensions to allow for free flow of movement, voice and creativity. By incorporating scientific understanding of the body functions into the creative process we hope to be able to give a firm basis to the imagination. This directly or indirectly will no doubt increase our own self confidence.

By learning the functions of the different parts of the body – head and neck, torso, pelvis, legs and arms – we can discover the relationship between the various parts and the body as a whole. This relationship can be expressed in varying individual rhythms.

To break through inhibitions while developing imagination, a part of the training is done through specifically directed improvisations. These are always preceded by physical preparations to make the body supple enough to express feelings spontaneously and truthfully. The floor is used as a source of strength. With proper awareness contact with the floor is of utmost importance. Secure strong feet are 'happy feet' carrying their owner safely through space. A well-elongated spine will carry the head freely and the body will 'float' easily. A correct movement is always aesthetically pleasing, and there exists no movement to which one cannot find some equivalent in the animal world, be it in a bird, a lion, a snake or a cat.

The ancient Chinese long ago recommended, as a means to long life, that men should 'pass some time like a dormant bear,' and 'imitate the flappings of a duck, the ape's dance, the owl's fixed stare, the tiger's crouch, the pawing of a bear'.

(*Chuang Tzu*, fourth century BC)

'Fatigue your body and you exhaust your mind' was an old Taoist maxim.

We strive for an emotional equilibrium, for reestablishment of the human communication that has been distorted by a mechanical age. We strive for *joi de vivre*, not the self-indulgence that springs from many modern misdirected efforts to cure ailing humanity. We create a synthesis of non-verbal communication – artistic perception – and awareness of the body.

Rhythm is an important factor. But in our method

movement is not necessarily dependent on or related to music and can be expressed independently. In the structure of movement we find analogies to musical concepts like legato – staccato, crescendo – decrescendo, canon, counterpoint and polyphony. To explore individual rhythms we work without music, and our classes are accompanied by music only for artistic reasons, for atmosphere, improvisation and choreographed movement.*

Just as sound is a spontaneous creation of human beings that – in the form of music – has created a highly complex language based on a universally accepted notation system, so movement is equally a spontaneous creation capable of developing a language of its own. We have accordingly integrated the concepts of understanding and analysing movement laid down by the Eshkol – Wachmann system of movement notation into our own work. This has enlarged our vocabulary and enabled us to define movement precisely.

Awareness of the Body – New and Old

We have been inspired by aspects and essences of several techniques. Each system has widened our understanding of the functions of the body as a whole and improved our ability to communicate the nature and source of movement to our students, but we don't preach a system or a method – we have developed ways of working.

1 **Moshe Feldenkrais†** has opened a total new approach to the understanding and development of movement, based on his experience as a physicist and mechanical engineer, using his scientific knowledge

---

* 'The question often arises, what can be the source and basic structure of my own dancing. I cannot define its principles more clearly than to say that the fundamental idea of any creation arises in me as a completely independent dance theme. The theme calls for its own development. It is in working this out that I find my dance parting company with the music . . . each dance demands organic autonomy'.
Mary Wigman, 'Composition in Pure Movement' from *Modern Music*, 1946.

† See 'Glossary of Integrated Concepts' and Bibliography: Feldenkrais, Moshe – Awareness through Movement.

and insight. His method works for economy of movement like the ancient T'ai Chi Ch'uan system of movement, that was guided by the principle that the exercise which is truly health-promoting must never exhaust or fatigue, but on the contrary should build up energy and produce a feeling of contentment. Maximum efficiency should be achieved by a minimum of effort, not through increased muscular strength but increased consciousness of *how* the body works. His work is directed at influencing the central nervous system. To reduce the restrictive, inhibitive controls from the forebrain, so that the reflex actions of the 'old' brain can organise the body on a level far deeper than can be achieved intellectually. This means re-establishing animal connections between instinctive emotional impulses and muscular reflex action, so that emotional energy can flow unblocked through a free body. Feldenkrais maintains that unity of mind and body is an objective reality; we feel with our bodies, and our behaviour patterns determine our feelings.

Moshe Feldenkrais works mainly on the floor to eliminate the antigravity response and free the muscles to change their patterns. He works on co-ordination, breathing, flexibility, freeing the joints to rotate with greater freedom. The pelvis with the strongest muscles attached to it is the source of power. It is in a sense the driving force of a person.

Every lesson is a separate unit dealing with one theme. This is developed from every possible point of view – one repeats and listens to one's own action many times. This technique is aimed at heightening the perception, always rechecking the influence of one isolated movement phrase on the functioning of the body as a whole.

One of his main methods is working on *one side* of the body, improving the performance and then comparing it to the side that has not worked. This enables one to realise the difference between improved and 'ordinary' functioning. Another way is to imagine the movement in the mind only, repeating it several times, then to do it again and check for improved movement ability.

Four factors determine every action: movement, sensory perception, feeling and thinking.

2 **Noa Eshkol** was influenced by Moshe Feldenkrais and has created a unique way of using the body in space, analysing and defining the essence of any movement; she has arrived (in cooperation with Abraham Wachmann) at a movement notation system able to describe with precision the maximum movement possibilities of the human body, irrespective of type or style. This is both a descriptive method and a tool for making dances, in analogy with composition in music.

Her analysis divides movements into three basic types:

a. Movement in a plane – horizontal or vertical – where the axis of the limb is at right angles to the axis of movement;

b. Rotation – in which the limb moves about its own axis without changing its place in space;

c. Conical Movement – in which the limb moves in a cone; its axis at an acute angle to the axis of movement.

The notation is written like a musical score. The body is considered for the sake of notation like an orchestra: the movements are chords in space.*

An important innovation in her system is the law of 'heavy and light limbs', which states that when a 'heavy' limb moves, it carries with it its appropriate 'lighter' limb. 'The terms 'light' and 'heavy' may therefore be used of any limb: they indicate whether the limb moves 'actively' or 'passively'. This law is not to be confused with the general feeling of heaviness and lightness in the body.

3 **The Alexander Technique** works on the relationship between the back, neck and head, the elongation of the spine, freeing contracted muscles and changing

* see Bibliography, Movement Notation – Eshkol-Wachmann.

faulty habits by way of tactile contact between one teacher and one student. Its five principles are:

1 To break faulty habits;

2 To inhibit from doing: meaning to learn to listen to our own body and discover which parts are unnecessarily tense;

3 Since most people's sensory perception is incorrect (they contract their muscles unnecessarily and waste valuable energy in moving), to teach the student the head-neck reflex, or 'primary control'. This is done by gentle manipulation so that the head is released, enabling the spine to elongate.

4 Through the elongation of the spine, to place the body in the correct direction 'forward and up', producing great lightness and ease of movement;

5 The idea of 'Primary Control' sums up the principles: Breaking bad old habits, inhibiting wrong contraction of muscles, pointing out correct behaviour patterns helped by personal touch, improving individual sensory appreciation until the student is able to use the body in a correct and healthy way, keeping the spine elongated without being rigid, breathing freely, accenting the importance of exhalation to create a vacuum in the lung enabling the diaphragm to move freely.

4 Recently we have also become involved in the **T'ai Chi Ch'uan** which we studied with Gerda Geddes in London, who in turn studied with an old Chinese master in China. It is an ancient Chinese system of 37 movements combined in large sequences into 108 forms, repeated always in the same order. It aims at achieving health and tranquility. Its movements are performed slowly and fluently without straining. The energy is controlled with awareness.

Its principles are harmony – balance – circular movement – stillness – circulation of the *Chi* energy – effortless effort. These are combined into phrases of poetic imagery, derived from the Taoist philosophers.

Each sequence tells its own story and finishes in the same position, 'The Bird's Beak'.

The system reflects the philosophy of the Yin and the Yang. Yin and Yang are universal forces. They symbolise the principle of dualism.

Yin – earth, passive, negative, female.

Yang – heaven, active, positive, male.

Between them exists a perpetual reciprocity, interdependence and correlation.

> 'To be' and 'not to be' arise mutually. Difficult and easy are mutually realised, Long and short are mutually contrasted . . . Before and after are in mutual sequence.

Stillness is considered the master of motion. When the harmony of the Yin and Yang is perfect, a bird can sit on your hand without being afraid.

The system works within the principles of correct use of the body: good breathing in tune with gravity forces, balance of the body in space, free-flowing movement aiming at the emotional and mental wellbeing of the performer.

Each of these systems has contributed to our awareness of the body and our attempts to achieve the sensation of freedom and lightness, release from superfluous tension, co-ordination and balance of the mind-body relationship.

We try to go *beyond defined dance styles* both in education and in work with professionals, by integrating various ways of working. By a real understanding of the structure and potentialities of the human body physically and expressively, and by concern with *how* to do, not only with what to do, we teach our students to move sensibly, to express themselves in a meaningful way, extending their personalities, not senselessly moving about. We want our students fully to enjoy their artistic experience by embracing both the technical basis and the artistic imagery.

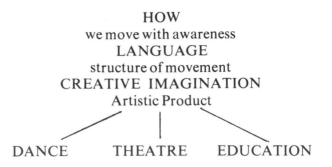

HOW
we move with awareness
LANGUAGE
structure of movement
CREATIVE IMAGINATION
Artistic Product

DANCE   THEATRE   EDUCATION

GLOSSARY OF INTEGRATED CONCEPTS

The concepts on which we base our work relate first of all to awareness of the body-mind relationship. They create the framework for daily actions and underlie every reasonable movement system. This is essentially a remedial approach to counteract misuse of the body: a good way to establish one's own neutral position, and to reduce superfluous tension. But our concepts can be useful for other techniques like Classical Ballet, Graham Technique, T'ai Chi Ch'uan, Vocal Systems and more. *How* the body works is a universal principle underlying any known technique.

ORGANISATION AND PROPER USE OF THE BODY

Spatial relationships

are relationships between different parts of the body: Head and neck in relation to the torso; torso in relation to the pelvis; pelvis in relation to the legs; and each of the above to all other parts of the body, bearing in mind their organisation around the vertical central line, and the 'law of heavy and light limbs',* which states that a moving limb carries with it the 'lighter' limb.

Co-ordination

is the orchestration of all or some parts of the body. The human being's most versatile contact with space is through the visual system, which is the most far-reaching and instantaneous form of perception. So co-ordination between the body and the rest of the world is mainly achieved through sight. Therefore it is essential

* As described by Eshkol-Wachmann in *Movement Notation* see Bibliography

12

	to co-ordinate body and eye movements. An organised body is capable of co-ordinating simultaneous movements of its different parts in various planes in space.
Antigravity mechanism	One of the vital functions of the body is to counteract gravity and this habit is maintained by the body in behaviour patterns.
	In our modern civilisation these patterns become distorted through bad use of the body (sitting on ill-constructed chairs, driving cars, lying on unsuitable beds). In order to re-educate the body and bring it back to its basic healthy functions it is best to start by eliminating the necessity to counteract gravity by working on the floor while lying or sitting.
Eutony*	We use the concept Eutony to mean the right amount of muscle tone needed for any movement: not too much and not too little. Too much tension is a waste of energy. Too little is a waste of another kind, it results in lack of vitality. So Eutony means a balancing of the muscular activity by releasing superfluous tension or increasing muscular tone in slack muscles.
Elongation	For maximum awareness of elongation of the spine one should be conscious of an imaginary cross behind one's back. The vertical line runs behind the spine and head; it is met by a horizontal line crossing the spine behind the shoulder-blades. These lines reach far beyond the body into infinity. One should be careful not to hold one's breath while imagining those lines.
Image of the body	We ought to be able to make a mental image of our own body and to describe in our imagination every part of it. We ought to feel its pressure, weight, balance, co-ordination and shape – the body in parts and as a whole.
Deliberate spontaneity†	This means to be ready for action in the full sense of the word. The body in a state of readiness should be in Eutony, not tenseness; it can be compared to the arrow

* The term used by Gerda Alexander from Copenhagen.
† Term derived from Moshe Feldenkrais.

in a bow. Readiness means the capability to react to any unexpected situation. By not being over-tense, readiness can be maintained virtually indefinitely without fatigue.

Reversibility* Proper use of the body means that any movement can be stopped and reversed almost instantaneously at every stage of its performance. We should be masters of our movement, being aware of what we are doing and not letting movements 'happen to us'. This is a quality of movement only attainable through a high degree of training.

Observing and absorbing* Work may be done on one part of the body only, for example one arm. After having worked on one arm, observe and compare both arms. The difference between the two limbs in lightness or heaviness should be clearly felt.

Lightness After going through the procedure for all parts of the body the final result should be a sensation of lightness, ease and serenity – without the use of drugs. In this state the body acquires its highest degree of readiness for any activity and is best capable of creative work.

Kinaesthetic awareness is awareness of one's own body while moving in space.

In a nutshell – to be aware and observe what one is doing is more important than mechanical frequent repetition.

*Terms derived from Moshe Feldenkrais.

Organisation and proper use of the body

derived from the ancient chinese
philosophy of the five elements

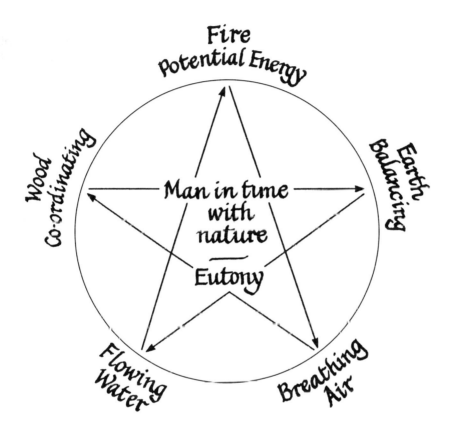

Fire
Potential Energy

Wood
Co-ordinating

Earth
Balancing

Man in tune
with
nature
—
Eutony

Flowing
Water

Breathing
Air

The Way of the Energy Flow

Flowing meets potential energy, controlling it;
potential energy meets breathing;
breathing meets coordinating;
coordinating meets balancing;
balancing meets flowing.

2   Basic Awareness of the Body

God guard me from those thoughts men think
In the mind alone.
He that sings a lasting song
Thinks in a marrow bone
                                    Yeats

AWARENESS OF THE ANATOMY OF THE BODY

If we want to use our bodies with maximum efficiency and minimum effort, we need to go step by step.

We need to re-educate people to be aware of their inborn but lost instinctive behaviour.

Therefore at first we want to acquaint ourselves with the raw material, our anatomical structure, and how to use it; and to relate this to the vital functions of the body.

A person who moves correctly is one who uses his body so that it suffers no superfluous tension or pressure in any part. There should be adequate room for all internal organs to function properly and for a good supply of blood to reach all systems requiring it.

Every man is a unique entity and will therefore differ from all others in the way he uses his body – but, however particular his body type, he should use his body according to the above principles, for he is the sole proprietor of his body and therefore responsible for its use.

Image of the Body

a. Visualisation

To make students think about the structure of the body and visualise it, we ask them to model a body in plasticine or other plastic material with eyes closed, or to draw it with open eyes.

Everyone then puts his figure in front of him and we all discuss our feelings about the work.

These are some of our own students' comments (these were first-term acting students).

'I am proud of him.'

'I spent hours working out the buttocks.'

'It was hard to get the proportions right, particularly the back.'

'I like working with closed eyes; I could concentrate and let the imagination flow.'

'I felt irritated.'

'I felt infuriated, frustrated, all the bones and muscles . . .'

'I wanted to show that it was moving.'

'They all look very primitive like totempoles.'

'I found it difficult to find the right proportion because I made the limbs separately and then the kneecaps.'

'I started with a whole piece and found the pivotal parts difficult, hard to put on muscles and flesh afterwards.'

'I found I had to exaggerate everything.'

'The head is not really necessary.'

'I first put her standing, then I found the feet were getting too heavy and I put her flat down.'

'Everybody made what they were not – tall people small figures and vice versa.'

'I was annoyed because I could not see what I was doing.'

'M. made a complete man from the wild west with gun, hat, cartridges.'

b. Scanning, sensing

Whilst lying on their backs we ask students to concentrate on the following:

Contact with the floor
Be aware of the pelvis, the centre of gravity. It is the strongest link in the structure, connected at one junction to the spine, upwards, and at the other to the legs, downwards at the hipjoints.

Check every part of the body for contact with the floor. Start from the legs upwards, step by step. Progress symmetrically, compare the feeling on right and left in relationship to the floor.

17

Relationship	Discover the relatedness and dependency of all parts of the body. Listen and develop a sense of flow. Listen to
Elongation	the elongation of the spine, feel the freedom of the head and neck.
Weight	Feel the weight of the tongue touching the lower front teeth. Feel the weight of the eyeballs inside the eye, move the eyeballs from side to side with closed eyes. It is also possible to press parts of the body to the floor, and release them.

This experience is one of the most important to bring about rest, release from tension and a feeling of peacefulness.

Structural Concepts.

The skeleton	The bones are co-ordinated to form the skeleton. Even in rest they depend on mutual support. Two kinds of bones are considered for our purpose:

The head, neck and trunk are single units, the legs and arms are pairs.

The motoric organisation leads from bone to muscle. The arrangements of the bones give shape to the body as a whole. The skeleton is jointed to allow movement. The movements are brought about by muscles, which are attached to the bones by ligaments and tendons. The muscles expand and contract, exerting a pull on the bones, which act as levers.

The vertebral column	The vertebral column is composed of thirty-three vertebrae, some of which are fused so that for our purpose there are twenty-four bones to be considered. They appear in the following arches:

Cervical curvature – 7 vertebrae
Thoracic curvature – 12 vertebrae
Lumbar curvature – 5 vertebrae

The sacral curvature consists of 9 vertebrae interconnected.

Joints	Experience shows us that every type of joint allows for a different amount and quality of movement.

| The ball and socket joint | gives free range of movement: in a plane, in conical movement or in rotation (using the terms of Eshkol- |

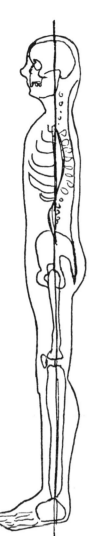

Correct Balance Line

The hinge joint	Wachmann movement notation) allows for movement in a plane up to 180°.
The pivot joint	the atlas and axis = head and neck – rotates 180° in the horizontal plane and participates in all other head movements with the vertebrae.
The gliding joints	are the vertebrae, ribs and knee caps.

Gravity is a force acting always downwards towards the earth in a vertical direction. For a well-organised body in a standing position, the pull of gravity can be traced in a straight line running through the ankle, hip joint, shoulder joint and the centre of the ear. Muscles act to counteract the pull of gravity. Therefore to be in tune with nature's force, a man must so organise himself that the distances between various parts of the body and the vertical line of gravity will be as small as possible, allowing for the natural curves of the spine. The organised body counteracts the forces of gravity by activating the muscles.

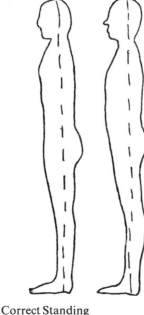
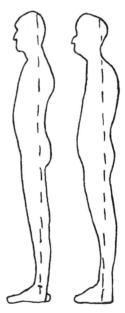

Correct Standing

19

Yin and Yang As everywhere else in nature, the law of opposites applies. The ancient Taoists called the interplay between the negative and positive the Yin and Yang. The Yin represents the negative, feminine, receptive, earth, darkness and night. The Yang represents the positive masculine, creative, light and day.

How can we improve our posture?

Correct posture is *not* a *static* concept. Correct posture is achieved by balancing the different parts of which the body consists. The bones are passive; they are kept in a correct relationship by the activity of the muscles.

Now we can begin to experience the relationship between the functions of bones and muscles. Muscles in order to function need to have a certain amount of tone. They work in opposing groups, contracting and decontracting in turn. In order to perform fully their function of flexing and extending they need to be kept flexible.

The body and the nervous system develop together under the influence of gravity so that the skeleton can keep itself upright without wasting energy.

In bad posture the muscles are called to replace part of the actions normally performed by the bones; by doing so they will waste energy and be prevented from performing their own function, that of moving the body in space.

One has to consider posture from the point of view of dynamics. Every stable balanced position is one of a succession of positions creating together a movement.

Posture experienced imaginatively.

By examining posture we become aware of the meeting point of the main vertical line going through the body, meeting the horizontal line going through the shoulder blades. Those lines are to be considered as part of infinity, and when working on these directions we stress the fact that we are part of our surroundings; they don't end in the body but extend into the periphery. It is important to accentuate the imaginative concept. We experience that the *image* of any *shape* contributes to improvement in the use of the body, and by doing so adjust the posture and co-ordination in movement.

How should we stand?

Neutral position Our contact with earth being by touching it with our feet, we discover that the best way for them to do so, whilst standing, is to distribute the weight among three points:

heel – big toe – small toe

using the foot as an arch, keeping the weight forward and up.

In neutral position we stand with feet parallel as far apart as the hips, arms hanging freely at the sides of the body, palms facing each other.

By a slight outward rotation of the hip joint, the feet will be helped and at the same time the pelvis will be balanced and ready for movement, a state of dynamic suspension.

The spine should be used at its maximum elongation, aiming at the natural space between each vertebra without hypertension. The balancing line of the body leads from ankle joint, through hip joint, through the head of the shoulder joint and through the centre of the ear, so in order to move well we have to pay attention to the relationship between head and neck, shoulders and the lower part of the body, the pelvis and legs.

The sensation will be of lightness, as though the back is far away from the legs.

How should we sit so that we can rise easily from a chair?

We should be able to get up without any excess tension and effort, enabling the anti-gravity reflex existing in the legs to function freely. Always think along the vertical line moving along the spine, and the horizontal line crossing the shoulder blades. Think of moving the head away from the shoulders, avoiding a hollow back. Separate the pelvis from the legs in your mind!

Sitting on a chair, put the whole foot on the floor, with the weight divided evenly between both legs.

To get up, the easiest way to begin with is by opening the legs widely, thinking in the direction of up and forward (it is possible to help oneself by pulling gently upwards on a strand of hair); whilst checking for complete freedom of the neck rotatory movement, and not holding the breath.

21

MOVEMENT AWARENESS

In the following pages we deal with parts of the body and their primary function, presenting 'raw material'. By working in an analytical way we deepen awareness and help to understand the functional relationships of the body – seeing a whole, separating it into its component parts, and putting it together again.

1 We start most lessons by running in one circle in a 'neutral' way. This makes one aware of one's whole body, improves the breathing and makes for a sense of group unity.
2 We work first on one side of the body, to sharpen awareness. This increases perceptiveness of the improved functioning of one part, and its influence on the rest of the body.
3 Scanning of parts of the body can be done at any stage, before or after any activity to release the body from superfluous tension and improve the self-image.
4 The principle of working in a static position is to go into depth – emphasising a special area of the body or a general theme – to make sure that experience is always accompanied by knowledge and awareness.
5 We each work to the point of our own ability, not straining to go beyond it; by repeating a movement within our own limit several times, we increase its range almost imperceptibly.

This chapter is intended as material for students to work on in their own way. The headings are not separate lessons.

We work towards developing continuous themes by building gradually along a guiding line, using concepts comparable to those of music: scales, themes and variations. We do not use unrelated exercises, but present ideas and concepts to work with. These seeds are developed into movement sequences, bearing in mind the underlying concepts of working:

Maximum efficiency with minimum effort; readiness to act without any preconditioning in any direction and to any purpose with the maximum free flow; there is no limit to improvement.

The Joints

Our purpose here is to encourage students to discover the units of the body physically by moving freely. The main units are the *head* and *neck*, the *torso*, the *pelvis*. The pairs are the *legs* and *arms*. The various units meet at the joints.

Many movements need the co-operation of several joints: describing a circle (cone) with the lower arm incorporates the shoulder and elbow joints; or the ballet *fouetté* needs the participation of the hip and knee joints.

We ask students to move the legs at the hip joints, the arms at the shoulders, and they usually come to the conclusion that

Definition

every movement is part of a circle.*

The body moves at its joints in order to change its presence in space or the relationship between its various parts.

Having discovered that every movement is part of a circle, we look for one joint that enables its limb to move a full circle – 360°. The shoulder is a ball and socket joint. The other ball and socket joint is the hip joint, but its movement is generally smaller because of its need to stabilise the body, the legs having to carry the weight of the pelvis and upper body.

Amount of movement

There are two different ways of looking at a circular movement. First there is the purely physical ability of movement of limbs in a joint; then there is the shape that the limb creates in space.

The elbow joint can move 180° only, but it is easy to draw a full circle in space with the lower arm. The latter is created by an interplay of action in the shoulder joint and the elbow; the shoulder joint rotates, while the elbow bends and stretches.

By experiencing movements one discovers that a similar process works in the knee joints.

We ask students to work for themselves and find the various movement possibilities:

* This idea is elaborated in the chapter on Space.

23

large circle – small circle; make combinations of large and small circles. Work in co-ordination, two arms at once, one arm moves in a large circle, the other in a small circle. Work at different speeds with differences in size with two arms.

Work on the same themes with one arm and one leg – differences in speed and size; work with two, three and four limbs; work with two and four limbs – symmetrically, as this is simplest; work with two and four limbs – parallel; work with two and four limbs – asymmetrically; make a sequence of repetitive movements in which the limbs work in an order from one to four, such as making a circle with right lower arm, adding a circle with left lower leg, then a circle with the left arm, but stopping the left leg from moving, then continuing with left lower arm, stopping the other arm. This phrase should be repeated at least three times.

No indication of timing is given by the teacher.

The following movements are designed for analysing and building at the same time, working in groups and moving in space. This type of work can be compared to practising musical scales and makes for flexibility and co-ordination of body and mind.

Divide a group into two:

One half works only on bending and stretching movements in varying quantities: 45°, 90°, 135°, 180°, with the joints of legs and arms. The other half works on movements of 90° only.

Movements of the head can be incorporated into sequences to add expressiveness and co-ordinate movements.

Change over the groups to enable everyone a turn at each experience.

Give each group the chance to watch the other.

Divide a group into smaller units of 2 – 5 people: the task remains to work in a set of movements, bending and stretching, creating angles of any quantity, creating a definite phrase that can be repeated for each group.

Work in couples: one person works on straight angles – bending and stretching in different quantities – the other person works on a circular movement that is a combination of bending, stretching and rotation.

The movements in this section can be varied to be performed standing, sitting and lying, either separately or combined in different ways.

Students prepare their *own compositions at home*

25

consisting of angular movements, circular movements, or a combination of both.

Students' own compositions at home should always consist of themes previously explored in class.
Following this type of work we usually suggest our students create an environment they like. And among the students' themes prepared at home we have received:
'In a test-tube'
'In a box with one window'
'An igloo'
'Being in Egypt'
'In a cardboard box'
'In an inflatable balloon'
'A lion in an arena'
'In a glass fishtank'
'In a ball'

Sitting

This section experiments with the concept of sitting.
Correct sitting on a chair.
Distribute the weight evenly on the 'sitting bones', ie the two protruding bones at the base of the pelvis. Place the feet on the floor, the space between them the width of the hips, feet and thighs pointed forward and parallel. The weight should be distributed equally on both feet.

Shift the weight from one edge to the other until a balance is found in the centre. The back should be lengthened without being strained, the head balancing freely on a long and free neck without curving the lumbar region.

Shift the weight forward and backward from the hip joint, keeping the back elongated. Roll the pelvis forward and backward to create either a concave or a convex shape in the back. Roll the pelvis in three stages:
backward-concave
centre – elongated, upright
forward lumbar curve – convex.

Sit correctly as specified above. Rotate the head from right to left and reverse, looking out for a precise horizontal view (following one straight line along the walls

of the studio, parallel to the floor, keeping the head away from the shoulders as far as possible). Throughout the head movement avoid hollowing the back. Combine the rotating movement of the head with the previous shift of weight of the pelvis.

Oriental position with crossed legs.

Various sitting positions

Check the position of the pelvis – the weight should be on 'sitting bones'. Roll from side to side. Check the position of the head – it should be balanced freely on long neck without superfluous tension. Roll, or rather shift the weight from side to side. Take care in every position not to contract the lumbar muscles – not to hollow the back. Lengthen the spine. Roll the pelvis forward and backward, or in the rhythm forward – centre – backward – centre.

Repeat the preceding actions in the following positions, sitting on the floor.

Symmetrical Open oriental position. Straight legs forward touching the floor. Legs open as far as possible, touching floor. Soles of feet touching each other (knees bent). Feet standing in front of the body (knees bent).

27

Asymmetrical Bend both legs to one side, separating the thighs so that the foot of one leg can touch the knee of the other leg. From the last position bring the back leg forward across the opposite thigh, putting the sole of the foot on the floor.

In all these positions repeat the distribution of weight and the correct positioning and relationship between the different parts of the body. Other positions can be explored – they will constitute variations on the basic theme.

Exploring the Back

The following work is done on three levels of perception:

a. clarifying and explaining the correct physical use of the body
b. discovering the many possibilities of moving the back
c. extending this awareness into imaginative concepts aimed at developing and encouraging creativity.

We endeavour to finish every lesson by a defined sequence of movement composed by students themselves from the elements introduced.

It is possible to arrive at a conclusion in two different ways:
1 Through pure movement sequences incorporating changes of positions and rhythm – slow and fast – staccato and legato – short and long.

Or

2 By a story-telling and imaginative approach: based on the natural elements – water – wind – fire. The animal world. The material world – clay – honey – shapes of rock.

Practical work

Standing

We tell students to stand with legs parallel, weight evenly distributed between both legs as described in 'neutral position'. From here we proceed with the following tasks:

We lead into the movements with a defined rhythm.

Let the head fall forward, become aware of its weight, let this weight pull after itself the rest of the spinal column until everything hangs forward and feels heavy, legs remain straight. Pay attention to the free hanging down of the head and neck, neck muscles must be untensed, breath not held. From this free hanging position start building the body back into its upright position as follows: start from the base of the spine (pelvic region), build upon it one vertebra on top of the other. The feeling must be that of unfolding the spine upwards. After arriving back at the standing position, shift the weight of the whole body forward and backward like a tree in the wind.

Now the same process is repeated in sections as follows: Release head and neck forward – return to upright position; Release head and neck and shoulders – return to upright position; Release head, neck, shoulders and torso – return to upright position; Release head, neck, shoulders, torso and pelvis – return in the same order: pelvis, torso, shoulders, head and neck to upright position.

Repeat the whole process in one movement, while producing a sound like: ssss, mmmmm, aaaaah, – by

29

making a sound we are sure to release instead of holding the breath.

Everyone now works to his own rhythm.

Catposition
Stand on all-fours; lower legs and hands touching the floor; thighs and lower arm vertical to the floor; space between arms equal to width of the shoulders, space between thighs equal to width of the hips.

All the following work will be done without moving the arms and legs from their position.

Move the pelvis forward and backwards: concave and convex. Think of curves as shapes. Move the pelvis forwards and back to centre (parallel to floor). Move the pelvis backward and back to centre (parallel to floor). Move the head and neck forward and backward (looking down to the floor and up to the ceiling) – concave and convex, thinking of the shape. Move the shoulders forwards and backwards – concave and convex. Make one large concave curve from the pelvis to the top of the head, then reverse into one large convex curve, moving the head and pelvis backwards and up towards each other.

Move shoulders and pelvis sideways towards each

other, without bending the elbow.

Widen the space between the arms by moving the hands sideways – this enables the muscles of the chest to work. Shift the weight of the whole body forwards and backwards to maximum, creating one large wavelike movement: one large circle making for maximum controlled flexibility. We start by one given rhythm and develop into variations with increased and diminished speeds.

Lying on the back

Students lie on their backs with bent knees, legs parallel, open to width of the hips.

Equivalent movement to the cat-position:

move the pelvis forward – concave – all the lumbar vertebrae come in contact with the floor; move the pelvis backwards – convex – enlarging the lumbar curve; move the shoulders forward – concave – backwards – convex; move the head and neck forward – concave – backward – convex; move head and neck and shoulders forward – concave – backward – convex. Bring the whole body into one flowing wavelike movement without stopping at any point: maximum flow and flexibility. Remain in the same position, weight distributed

31

evenly between both feet and shoulders, lift from the lowest part of the back one vertebra after the other until the weight rests on the shoulders – body straightens to one diagonal line – check that there is no pressure exerted on the neck by rolling the head from side to side. Return to lying flat on the floor by letting go one vertebra after another starting from the shoulders; pelvis arrives last. Repeat the movements many times until a free flow is created.

When returning from the lifted position the student may let the head and neck come forward and upward until arriving at a sitting position – all the time working on the free flow.

It is possible to achieve a straight line going through the whole body in a weightless movement by the following exercise: lie flat on the floor, knees bent, feet touching the floor, heels underneath the knees. Press into the floor with the feet only thinking of a diagonal line going down into the floor. In this way the spine stretches first before the pelvis lifts itself upwards.

The student can balance the weight of the body on different parts of the back to enhance his consciousness of the flexibility and strength of the back.

Lying on the back shift the weight of the body on to the lower back. Shift the weight onto the shoulders only. Try various different parts of the body, allowing for asymmetrical positions.

Possible sequences are from lower back – onto one or two shoulders – onto one side of the pelvis – rest. From these many variations can be found.

Be aware that one part of the back can carry the weight of the body while other parts are lifted off the floor.

Angles and
curves

Sit on a chair – open legs, feet touching the floor.
Lift head from the spine as far as possible without hollowing the back.

Starting from the sitting position, incline the back forward from the hip joint – creating one straight line – and backward to upright position. Move as far as possible and return, then repeat the same with one stop half way. (It can be 90° or 45°). In the same sitting position, bend the back in a curve forward leading from the head, go as low as possible, and on returning to upright position lead from the pelvis and straighten the back as soon as possible.

Combinations of straight lines and curves:
Start forward on a straight line, return on a curve in one wavelike movement. Start with a curved line forward returning with a straight line in one wavelike movement. Incline the back forward, in one straight line, stopping at 45° or 30° intervals; curve and straighten the back at each stop.

All the above movements can be done sitting on the floor in various positions – the easiest are:
sitting on the lower legs pelvis touching the heels (the back is free to move); sitting with both legs to one side, asymmetrical position – the movement will be done to the sides, changing the position from one side to the other.

33

How can we walk?

At first we define how we should walk. This is followed by experiencing walking in many ways.

Correct walk

Walking is transferring the weight of the body in space – actually every step is catching a forward fall. We prepare the thigh to be ready to take the weight of the body ahead of the pelvis by loosening the knee joint. The centre of gravity should be kept close to the central balancing line of the body. The correct movement involves rolling the weight of the body over the arch of the foot from the heel to the ball of the foot supported by big toe and small toe.

Preparation

To begin with we ask students to stand in 'neutral position' and shift the weight forward and back to centre several times. This changes the angle between the lower leg and the foot. It is helpful to pull a small strand of one's own hair up and forward. The whole body is thus elongated, and the gesture strengthens the feeling for the axis of the body.

We ask students to walk slowly at first, then to accelerate to fast walking; walk in different directions; walk by putting weight on the heels only; putting weight on the ball of the foot only; on the outside of the foot only; by putting weight alternately on the heels and the ball of the foot, preparing the big toe and small toe to support and balance the weight of the whole body.

We usually start by working first and analysing later.

Experiments

We ask students to experience walking, leading with one part of the body:

the elbow, the chin, the forehead, one shoulder, the chest, the pelvis.

Dramatic interpretation

Divide a group into small sections. Each one chooses to lead with one part of the body – imagining the character behind it and the direction the person would walk in. The time element determines the character and the purpose of the walk.

Walking on different surfaces:

On thistles, mud, stones, hot sand, loose earth, pitch –

one person being stuck, the others trying to free him, getting stuck as well.

Walk in:

a forest, a cave, through water, in the dark – how people can lose and find each other.

Walk and carry:

a basket filled with shopping; flowers to be given to someone; a small child; an umbrella in the wind.

Walk away from:

a soldier joining the army, a burning house.

Walk towards:

someone dear – a new girl friend; a new job.

Off-balance   Walk losing your balance:

being drunk, being a toddler,

in a gale.

Group activity   Everyone goes his own way – gradually joining other members of the group in twos, threes and more, until the whole group walks together in one way. No rhythm is dictated – the leaders change – everyone in his own character.

Bending – Lifting – Carrying

We allow students to work in their own way and we analyse afterwards every individual's use of himself. We explain that every lifting action should be done only by bending the knees and lowering the pelvis, using the strong muscles of the pelvis and thighs, *not by bending the back* unnecessarily. In other words, the hip joint allows the back to change its position.

Start by standing in neutral position. Bend the legs without lifting the heels (ankle and hip action). Pay attention to the relationship between knee and foot: it should be possible to draw a straight line from the centre of the knee to a point between the big and second toe. Bend in the following positions:

1 feet parallel touching each other;
2 feet open at width of the hips;
3 legs open to a wide position.

This is a good opportunity to learn the concept of *plié* from the Classical Ballet terminology, and the

35

'Monkey Position' from the Alexander Technique, stressing the correct relationship between the back and the legs and the freedom of the neck-head movement.

Bending and lifting

We use balls of paper to enliven the technical work, but insist on precise use of the body relationship as stated in the introduction.

Make balls of various sizes from newspaper – throw them and catch:
  Throw and catch close to the floor.
  Throw and catch far away from the floor.
  Roll the balls over the floor, lift off the floor.
  People watch each other, clarify the difference between various movements, like lifting with knees bent or straight.

Bending and lifting as dramatic themes

Lift an imaginary heavy weight. Lift an imaginary light weight. The whole group stand in a circle and hand to each other imaginary objects of various weights. Transfer from light to heavy and vice versa. Lift fine articles and make very clear what is being lifted, what is its

weight and what the texture is like. Possible choices: needle – thread – breadcrumbs – a feather – dust – beads – a hair.

Work in couples:
Lift an article, transfer it to another person, but drop it on the way so that the next person has to cope with the dropped article, which may be broken, damaged or changed.

Teamwork   Transfer a pole, a trunk, a sack of potatoes, an electric cable.
Make a sequence or a story from the various articles lifted:
'The Feather'
'A box of beads fallen down'
'A necklace breaks'
'A hair in the soup'.

Breathing
(*a*) *The importance of breathing*
According to the Bible man without breath would be

37

only a lifeless lump of earth, for God created man from earth and breathed into his nostrils the breath of life. Through this breath Adam became a living soul. Life means rhythm. With its first breath the new-born baby enters into the rhythm of life, exhaling – giving, inhaling – taking, the perpetuum mobile of life.

Primitive man who lived under natural conditions did not need to be taught how to breathe. Hunting, fishing, struggle against the elements and the upheavals of the weather, and constant movement in open air provided abundant natural exercise and made him instinctively a good breather. If we lived a normal natural life, our bodies and lungs would show the same sound reaction to outside influences as in primitive man. But in our civilisation we spend the greater part of our lives in badly ventilated rooms, sitting on unsuitable chairs, bending over badly aligned writing desks, sleeping on soft unsuitable beds. We become people with sunken chests, narrowed shoulders and badly placed heads and necks.

A whole range of negative emotions finds expression in the generally lessened tone of the dorsal extensors. Accordingly there will be compensatory hypertonicity of the flexors, which causes restricted breathing. This creates a vicious circle: we close in as a dramatisation of our feelings of fear, grief and anger, our muscle tone changes accordingly and our structure acquires destructive behaviour patterns. As a result we do not make use of our full lung capacity, depriving our organism of much of the oxygen needed for its full functioning . . .

Most muscles of the respiratory system are connected to the neck and lumbar vertebrae, therefore breathing of necessity influences the stability and mobility (general use of) the spine. Equally, a correctly balanced posture will influence the quality of the breathing. Therefore we may say that a good posture produces good breathing and good breathing will produce good posture.

Our breathing rhythm changes with our emotional states and our different activities: with anxiety or pleasure, or with the effort of doing something in a hurry, or lifting a heavy weight. If therefore we can use our breathing to its full potential and with even rhythm, we can heighten our general vitality.

Breathing is normally a reflex action whose rate varies with body activities, but it can to a certain extent be controlled voluntarily.

Inspiration, or breathing in, is brought about by
(a) lowering of the diaphragm, which increases the volume of the thorax, and
(b) contraction of the intercostal muscles, which swings the ribs outwards and upwards and thus increases the diameter of the thorax.

Both movements combine to increase the capacity of the thorax and thus suck air into the lungs through the respiratory passages. The air drawn in mixes with the air already in the lungs, so the air inside the lungs is never as pure as the air inhaled.

Expiration, or breathing out, is brought about by elastic recoil, when muscles relax.

Without a free flow of breathing there can be no free flow of energy in the body. With the free flow comes harmony of body and mind, the active and the passive: active the exhalation, passive the inhalation. Just as a bottle when full cannot take in any more fluid, and has to be emptied first to be refilled, so when the breath is held no movement is possible. As a corollary, no well performed movement should impede the breath.

(b) *Work on breathing*
A session opens with an all-group activity.

Running in a circle is a good way to start.

The weight of the body must be directed forward and up.

The foot should touch the floor with the ball of the foot then with the heel – we say 'run on the whole foot'.

Arms are passive, hanging freely on the sides of the body, the elbows are free, the wrists are free, the shoulders bounce freely.

The neck is long without superfluous tension.

The tongue rests inside the lower jaw, touching the lower front teeth.

The shoulders are far removed from the ears without being rigid.

The whole body bounces off the floor by the correct use of the concept 'forward and up'.

Use the momentum created by the running force and receive the push given by the floor.

Exhale rhythmically.

With practice this kind of running becomes second nature to students and we use it as an opening for most lessons.

One should not interfere with the individual breathing rhythm of students and not demand a unified rhythm of exhalation. From our experience we learned that eventually a well-trained group will reach a harmonious rhythm on its own.

The work described here can greatly help in producing good postural alignment. When working on the floor it is easy after a short while to feel the vertebrae between the shoulders touching the floor – a place that often seems almost numb before we work on it consciously. The linking of exhalation to the flowing movement from standing to lowering on to the floor and back (1) relaxes too selfconscious preoccupation with the breathing process only, and enables the student eventually to forget about thinking about breathing at all, so that his consciousness does not interfere with a natural breathing rhythm.

Working while lying on the floor

We proceed to work while lying on the back. Heels are kept underneath the knees, feet standing as far apart as the width of the hips. The soles of the feet touch the floor. Be careful at all times not to hollow the back, that is not to lift the lumbar vertebrae. The arms are lying at the side of the body, palms touching the floor, elbows slightly further away from the body than the hands. This may cause slight tension in the shoulders which will recede in time.

The natural way is to breathe in and out through the nasal passages. Through atmospheric pressure air will always enter into the lungs passively, therefore we work mainly on exhalation to make room for more fresh air. In order to gain control over exhalation and extend its duration, we usually work on exhalation with open mouth and sounding ssss, aaaah, mmmm etc. Or we may use words and songs in movements.

Breathing Exercises
The following exercises should not be used too many at one time. They vary with the condition and standard of a group.

Practical
breathing

a. Exhale with an sss sound – air is pressed through the teeth. Everyone uses his or her own basic rhythm, eventually extending the time of exhalation.

b. Exhale, mouth wide open, soft palate flexible, making a sound aaaah or haaa without voicing it, just a whispered breath.
Put the palms of the hands on the abdomen to follow its lowering and rising.

c. Exhale. Put the hands on the rib cage, the thumb touching the back of the ribs, the palms in front. Feel the up and outward movement of the lower ribs while inhaling, the down and inward movement while exhaling. Beware not to hollow the back!

d. Exhale, putting the thumb below the clavicle, feeling the lowering and rising of the top of the lungs.

e. Exhale, putting the palms of the hands on the back of the ribs, the thumb on the front ribs. Follow the three-dimensional movement of the rib cage.

f. Listen to the three-part rhythm of the breathing as follows: lower the diaphragm, to lift the abdominal muscles and thus extend the volume of the rib-cage so that air finally enters the tip of the lungs; lift the diaphragm, to pull in the abdominal muscles, push the air out of the lower lungs and draw it out of the upper lungs – thus creating a three part wave-like rhythm.

g. Exhale, hold without letting any air in from the outside, and push the diaphragm down and up 4–5 times; then be aware that yet more air will come out, then flow freely in and out. This exercise is like cleaning a bottle by shaking a small amount of water inside it.

h. Exhale by pushing the abdominal muscles upward and out while doing so.

   Most animals use this *paradoxical* way of breathing whilst roaring or howling: by enlarging the volume of the abdomen whilst exhaling they can create a very loud sound. In the Far East it is customary to practise this exhaling, paradoxical though it may be. It is assumed that one gains greater control of one's organs than in customary breathing, and improves the use of the spine. As a matter of fact we all use this paradoxical breathing when called upon to make a sudden effort.

i. Breathe by consciously directing air into one lung only. Start with the right lung, because it is the larger of the two. Put the palm of the left hand on the right side of the thorax. By concentrating on one side only, we can greatly improve the performance of our breathing, and become aware of the difference between the side that has been active as opposed to the one that has been passive.

Standing on hands and lower leg – cat position

j. The teacher puts the palms of his hands on the back of the student, below the small ribs. Let the student push the air against the slight pressure of the hands, thus sensitising the lower part of the thorax.

   When this has been experienced successfully, students may work on each other in couples: one active, one passive.

Work in couples

k. 1 One person sits with crossed legs, the other puts his hands on the sitting person's back, feeling the vibrations of the breathing process on different spots.

2 Sit back to back, the whole back touching, sound *hmmm* simultaneously and alternately, feel the vibrations on as wide an area as possible. In the same way let the backs of the head touch each other, feel the humming sounds vibrate through the heads and into space.

3 Stand in neutral position. Send the humming voice through the body into the legs or into the arms. Check with each other whether the vibrations can be felt by touching the outside of the limbs.

Breathing while moving

1. Stand, and let the body fold down to the floor and come back to standing position on *one* exhalation process. Exhale with one long ssss or hmmm sound. With growing experience it is possible to enlarge the range of movement by creating wavelike movements, or by going down and coming up twice on one breath.

3 Sensory perception

What does a child learn?
The island of his name and body
Against the increasing strangeness of the world
Dennis Silk

TOUCH –
SOUND –
SIGHT

We all see, hear, speak and touch; and with the same organs we use for these functions we also co-ordinate movement, balance ourselves, taste and breathe – so we have to explore these areas in our own way.

We want to see more, to hear more and be more aware; we open ourselves to ourselves and to a heightened perception of the world around us.

We work with eyes closed to achieve a higher degree of concentration and awareness. At the moment of pinpointing our attention to the specific we discover more particulars, even in phenomena with which we have been acquainted for ages.

Usually we take many things for granted without really knowing them thoroughly.

We learn to trust and know ourselves and the people we work with; we also learn to react to varying situations, gaining a deeper insight into our own world and character.

We close our eyes and listen to our inner sounds – we become conscious of the rhythms of our breath and of our pulse; we close our eyes again – we feel the pulse in the upper and lower jaw, maybe in the eyes also; we close our eyes again – the spine seems to be pushed upwards like a plant; the joints suddenly come alive.

Having sharpened our senses to our inner self, let's listen to our surroundings – discovering innumerable sounds we didn't know existed: the clock suddenly pounds away, a dripping tap beats irregularly, the rain bombards the window and roof, the sounds of the cars passing the house make a whole symphony – modern music now makes much more sense.

45

LOOKING AND SEEING

To begin with we close our eyes and describe the immediate surroundings.

We shall be surprised at the different opinions as to how many windows there are in the studio, how many doors, pillars, how many heating elements, lighting elements, wall plugs, how many chairs, pianos, tape recorders etc.

What is made of wood or metal or plastic?

What colour are the tiles, walls and curtains?

Where are all these items located in the room?

Now sitting in a circle, glance for two seconds around you. Close the eyes: what colour shirts or trousers can you remember. To whom do they belong?

Glance around again for two seconds.

Close your eyes: who wears jewellery and what kind is it?

Describe everything you remember.

Glance around again.

Don't move, and describe people's positions; do they have legs crossed, open, bent, straight? If possible describe the mood of the people around you.

ORIENTATION

Walk around the room and look. Make yourself acquainted with the space.

Then with eyes closed go to a specified place (such as the wall, the barre, the door, the piano) and return to the place you came from as precisely as possible.

Open the eyes and talk about your various experiences. Comments made in our classes have included:

'Going to the wall was insecure because I was not sure of the distance to be covered. On the way back I was much more assured and could therefore walk faster.'

'I counted my steps in the first phase and on my way back knew exactly what to do.'

'I was frightened and afraid to bump into people.'

'I tried to listen to other people's steps.'

Next we repeated the experiment, this time putting obstacles in people's paths (e.g. chairs, rostra, sticks, pieces of clothing, balls).

Some comments were:

'I was much more careful than before.'

'On my way to the wall there was a chair that did not seem to be there when I returned.'

A variation: put various different types of obstacles in place, let people glance at them for 2–3 seconds, then ask them to close their eyes and try to avoid the obstacles or cross over them.

Development

To achieve confidence with eyes closed and sharpen kin-aesthetic awareness, people spread out in the room holding hands and close their eyes. We ask them to form a circle in the centre of the room and not to open their eyes until asked to do so. Similarly we ask the group, with eyes closed, to form:

Holding hands

    a straight line,

    a square,

    a triangle.

Without holding hands

Another way is to come with closed eyes into a circle, and sit down.

This kind of work leads to group conversation and lively exchange of individual experiences and feelings. It is best to work in two groups so that each can observe the other, and have both the active experience of doing and the passive experience of watching.

INNER VISUALISATION

We close our eyes while *lying on the back*; we imagine the exterior shape between our head and shoulders – it is triangular.

We draw an imaginary line between the head and our palms – it also is triangular.

Between the pelvis and the feet we can draw another triangle.

Now let's think of all three triangles at once – is it possible?

Now let's take an imaginary paint brush and fill in the triangular frames with different colours.

Try again to think of all three triangles at once; is it easier now?

Now let's draw lines between the shoulders – palms and feet – repeat several times: shoulders – palms – feet, palms – shoulders – feet, or shoulders – feet – palms.

Fill those last two triangles with paint: at first paint both triangles the same colour, then paint each triangle in a different colour.

After each experiment compare the size and the weight of the triangles.

Now bring both triangles to an equilibrium if possible.

Now make lines and shapes of your own.

Can you feel some more parts of your body easily and at once?

In a very short span of time people doing this exercise achieve serenity, are rested, light, and like to talk about their experiences.

Moving in space The following experiences are presented in two stages: the first to achieve the special sensation of concentrating in a static position; the second to develop this sensation by moving with the same awareness with open eyes in space.

This approach is very often used when working with actors on character studies – it produces amazing results very quickly, especially when an actor has to act a character of an age greatly different from his own.

Begin by standing with parallel legs, in 'neutral position'. Close your eyes and shift the weight forward and

49

backward without lifting any part of the foot.

Imagine the body consisting of *bones* only, that is imagine yourself to be a skeleton.

Describe the particular sensations.

The outcome of this will be that the muscular inhibitions will disappear, as far as imaginative work can influence our behaviour.

Next try the same experiment, imagining you consist of *muscles* only.

The movements will mainly involve contraction and release, as this is what muscle function is. Movements will take on a heavier and more sensuous character.

Last in the sequence imagine yourselves to consist of *skin* only.

Imagine that your whole body is covered by a giant glove, and become very conscious of the folds and creases made in the skin by moving. You will also become very much aware of the need to use the spine at its utmost elongation, otherwise you leave unwanted creases in the skin of the back and the abdomen.

STIMULATION OF THE SENSES – SENSE MEMORY

Take a number of different materials, such as velvet, silk, linen, wool, vinyl, nylon, fur, and put all the pieces in one heap.

Working with closed eyes, students sit in a wide circle, the materials in the middle.

Each person touches the various pieces, eventually picking up two pieces of different qualities.

Each tries to translate into movement the feel of the pieces of material, first of one, then the other, then the two, with different parts of the body. Students are free to move sitting, lying, standing or in a combination of these.

Students start moving in space.

They are told to form small groups (of 2–5 each), still with eyes closed. They are told by the teacher to move in simulation of a material of the teacher's choice. (Some will be those that they have just touched and some they will have to produce from their own sense-memory). They make their own sounds to equal the sensation, working in contrasts first, like silk and vinyl.

Combine the movement and the sound.

It is advisable, if the group is large enough, to divide the class into two halves, letting each watch the other.

After this experience one should let students paint or draw their experiences, expressing at least three different kinds of material.

TOUCHING

Working in couples with eyes closed

Choose a partner, with eyes closed.

Find a spot in the room, and start either sitting or standing. Touching each other with hands and arms only, make yourself acquainted with your partner in various ways: examine the *quality* of the skin, the contours of bone, assess the *character* of your partner – his strength or weakness, is he domineering, yielding, inquisitive, receptive?

Change positions when wanted, or change partners.

After the experience students talk about their reactions.

Some of our own students' comments were:

'I enjoyed that.'

'It was an excuse for violence.'

'I was totally concentrated to the exclusion of everything else.'

'Some hands are aggressive, like women's lib.'

'Standing up for yourself, always sensual – que sera, sera.'

'Some actors in the theatre always have the same hand gestures, they should have had this kind of experience.'

'One discovered a lot how skin feels.'

'How different muscles work.'

'The inside of the arm is sooo sensitive.'

'You can feel even the wind hands make.'

Variation:

Go through the same actions, then paint your experience on paper with colours, using any type of watercolour, oil crayons, pastels, felt pens. Then talk about your mutual experience and exchange reactions with the whole group.

51

TOUCHING AND TRUSTING

With eyes closed the whole group forms a circle, touching each others hands. Moving the arms and hands only, the circle as a whole can move in space and can become smaller or larger.

If the group is large enough it can be divided into two, so each can watch the other.

Each group's tasks are defined slightly differently, so that some, for instance, hold hands and move using high and low dimensions, which will make people bend and stretch their legs, thus exploring the vertical planes.

Comments made by students after working:

'I relied on my neighbour and let him lead me.'

'On my left the person was aggressive and tried to dominate me, on my right the person I was in touch with was passive.'

'I wanted to lead the movement but met with resistance and finally gave in.'

'I wanted to lead, my neighbour tried to prevent me, but I insisted and finally was in control.'

'The three of us were in total harmony.'

One of the most exciting classes we ever held consisted of fine art and drama students. They went into the experience of working with closed eyes with enormous enthusiasm and turned it eventually into an exuberant celebration, moving and dancing wildly to an enormous variety of rhythms and sounds produced by members of the group themselves. Nobody opened his or her eyes for over an hour. When they were asked what they felt, they said they were ecstatic and excited. When they were asked whether they minded not being able to see, they answered that the group gave them sufficient security.

Comments made by people watching some of the classes included:

'This was an exceptionally beautiful choreography.'

'It looked like a lot of strength and gentleness mixed.'

'It was like a sea, changing from rough to calm.'

'I found it hard not to join in.'

'I have never before seen my colleagues move with such freedom.'

53

'In our art classes we are never able to touch anyone apart from our girlfriend.'

'It reminded me of my childhood.'

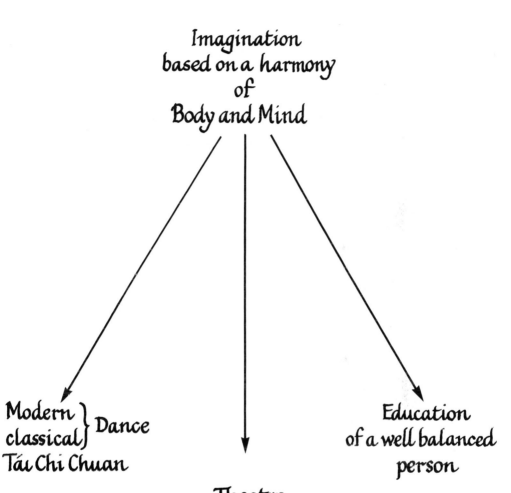

Imagination
based on a harmony
of
Body and Mind

Modern ⎱ Dance
classical ⎰
Tái Chi Chuan

Theatre
Visual Arts
Musicians

Education
of a well balanced
person

4 Imagination and Creativity

What the imagination seizes as beauty must be truth –
whether it existed before or not.

Keats

As people we exist on different levels, so we communicate in various ways, as a kaleidoscope in changing the relationship between various shapes creates an infinity of visions.

To inspire the imagination we work with the following ideas:

1 **The visual aspect**
Drawing the dot, the straight line and the curve;
painting with colours;
creating shapes with a rope;
using materials such as newspaper and cloth to change the shape and character of the body;
working with elastic material, creating shapes, co-ordinating and balancing movement.
In this way we extend the perception by relating to shapes outside our own body and enriching the inner image, so as to open up a fountain of free-flowing movement.

2 **Sense-memory and feeling**
We work from memory and imagination using the verbal imagery of colour to evoke associations, as well as using verbal imagery about objects, beginning with individual responses and developing a common theme for the whole group.

3 **Discovery of geometrical shapes**
Precise awareness of shapes – triangle, circle and square – individually and in relation to the whole group.

4 **Developing a character in a restricted situation**
Using various sitting positions; for instance, create characters at different times of their life in various locations, wearing different clothes.

5 Emotional response creating movement compositions and relationships between people
The story of a poem.

COLOUR, SHAPE AND MOVEMENT

The dot, the straight line, the curve (circle)

'By contemplating the optical-physical appearance the ego arrives at intuitive conclusions about the inner substance' – Paul Klee.

Following Paul Klee's idea of defining shapes we apply the principle of the dot, the straight line and the curve to create movement patterns with the body that can also express human feelings.

Use of drawing

Everyone takes a sheet of paper and draws any desired shape using *dots* only.

The drawings are put on the floor, everyone moves according to the drawn shapes, coming as closely as possible to the motif of dots, that is making staccato-like movements best produced by

skipping

using the fingers in the air or touching the floor

using the feet and toes while sitting on the floor.

Exchange the paintings to enable everyone to interpret someone else's painting.

Everyone takes a new sheet of paper and makes a drawing with *lines* only. The drawings are put on the floor and interpreted by creating linear movements only, using different parts of the body. Attention is paid to the rhythm of the lines and the contrast to the dotted shapes.

Work in couples:

Take one painting, one person interpreting it in standing position, the other doing the same sitting or lying, or combining both.

Variations:

Two people, one working on dots, the other working on lines.

Various sized groups, two, three, four or more

people, each group using either one, two or three paintings, either all in dots, all in lines or a combination of the two.

Divide a large class into two groups, fairly equally sized, and one does lines, the other dots.

Make a drawing using all three elements: the dot, the

Move the drawn motif in space, using the whole body, but paying special attention to the extremities. The centre of the body, the pelvis and the torso should initiate the movements while the arms and legs continue the flow of the shapes. The eyes should follow the patterns.

Make a drawing using all three elements: the dot, the line, the curved line.

Everyone interprets his own drawing:

with one arm only,

with the head and eyes only,

with one arm and one leg,

with three parts of the body.

Now the whole group stands in a circle, everyone's painting in front of him, people work one after the other, showing their own creation using different parts of the body, but not more than two at a time.

Put one painting in the centre of the circle, and one after the other interprets the same painting using only one part of the body, according to his own choice.

Divide the class into small groups of 2–5 people each: at a given sign one group moves at a time to a chosen spot, then another group joins it. When it reaches the spot the group freezes in a position, so that an interesting live sculpture is created; each group chooses whether it wants to move in curved or straight lines, or dots.

Variations are possible with the addition of appropriate sounds, like singing in legato or staccato, accenting one vowel or syllable. Percussion instruments can also be used.

Painting with colours

This is a technique for developing a particularly sophisticated way of communication. Students give of themselves in their painting, create names and participate in a communal effort which in turn is to be recreated in movement, thus enhancing their artistic perception and using their bodies expressively at the same time.

One person paints a colourful picture. His partner moves in space, following the motifs: using one limb for each colour – arms, legs or head, using the pelvis and the torso only.

Two people work on one page, each using his own colours, painting like a conversation, complementing each other; then they leave the painting, and try to express the contents of the conversation in movement.

Take one large roll of paper and put it in the middle of the studio. Everyone in turn adds a motif to the painting thus creating a large group picture. This should be done quickly in rotation. Everyone gives a name to the picture. The class is divided into small groups, and each group makes up a story for one of the suggested titles and enacts it in movement.

Variation: the finished painting is divided into four or five pieces, and each group is given one section to interpret as a group movement.

Materials to change the shape and character of the body

Newspapers
There are many possibilities hidden in a bunch of throwaway newspapers. They can be used to make
   1 Paperballs
   2 Shelter
   3 Clothes that make the person (different characters emerge).
   4 Or one can make use of the printed information.

Paper balls

1 Form balls of different size from the newspaper. Every person starts by playing with a paperball he has made for him/herself.

Use of breathing

When people have become acquainted with the material we start giving instructions.

Put the ball on the palm of the hand – blow on it to

move it first from one palm to another.
Move it from one person to another.
Put the ball on the floor – move it along the floor by blowing on it.
Divide into small groups using only one ball for each group – pass the ball from one person to the next.
Increase the distance between the people to extend the time of exhalation.

Balance

Move the ball across the floor using the feet only: by touching the ball with the toes only; by touching the ball with the heels only; by gliding the ball from toes to heels.

Use of the hip joint

Leave the heel on the floor, let the ball be moved by the outside part of the foot while opening the hip joint, making a gliding movement.
Leave the heel on the floor and glide the ball with the inside of the foot.

Sitting on the floor

Kick the ball from one person to another with both feet, sitting on the base of the pelvis only (the 'sitting bone'), keeping the back straight.
Kick the ball in the same way as before but balance the body on one side of the pelvis.
Move the ball across the floor touching it with different parts of the body:
   head,
   finger tips,
   elbows,
   lower arms.
Everyone takes one ball and throws it in different ways, catching it:
as high as possible,
as low as possible,
sitting on the floor,
lying on the floor.

Shelter

2 Spread the newspapers flat on the floor in many layers.
Suggest various situations to the group:
shelter from heat, rain, hail;
shelter in war; face to face with an enemy (shield);
attack from the air;
exploding bomb;
celebrating a happy event:

wedding,
anniversary,
national holiday (flags);
morning;
night.

Clothes that make the person

3 Every person takes as much paper as he/she wants to make into different types of clothing: the paper may be torn or cut to individual taste.

Eventually everyone assumes the character to fit his clothing.

Various situations will be suggested:
Carnival
Medieval pageant – Mummers' plays
a scene at court
a circus
a scene on a seashore
fashion show
fancydress ball.
Relate the characters and clothes to famous pictures – Breughel, Rembrandt, Goya, Velasquez, Boticelli; use a picture still – in motion and conversation – still again.

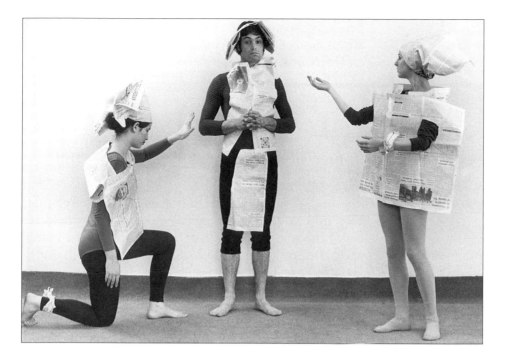

Use of printed information

4 Everyone looks at a page for its written content, chooses a line, a word, a short story, a news item, a cartoon or an advertisement.

At first everyone works for him/herself.

A small group uses one item to produce a situation, then another group develops the situation and may thus change the meaning of it.

Use only the title of a paragraph for an action.

Many variations can be found, and in general a group will fit the action to its own dynamic and character.

Prepare large coloured faces from illustrated newsprint. Bring scissors and rubber bands to make masks from the pages. Cut out the outlines, if necessary stick them on to cardboard, fix the rubber bands to fit over ears. Give these masks to people and let them assume the character of these.

Here is one way to work in couples. Give each person a certain mask without showing him the face, and don't use mirrors. Place the two people opposite each other and let them create the character from a conversation developing between the two, so that everyone has to create his own character from the other person's questions and reactions.

Work with elastic

Every student is asked to bring a loop made of elastic ribbon, half an inch wide and about 2½–3½ yards long, according to the height of the student, to be held between the soles of the feet and the palms of the hands, while the arms are stretched high to exert a pull on the limbs to be resisted.

We suggest work with elastic material because it creates interesting shapes, while at the same time forcing people to co-ordinate their movements, thus enriching the imagination while working on the technical improvement of motion.

Lying on the floor

Start by lying on the back: put the elastic between the thumb and the palm of the hand and the soles of the feet at a point where it is easy to grip (inside the arch of the foot).

Try to lift both legs and arms straight off the floor while gripping the elastic. If this is difficult, proceed as follows:

Lift the arms alternately, keeping them straight, putting one arm back on the floor before lifting the other.
Lift both arms and head.
Lift the legs alternately keeping them straight.
Lift right arm and left leg.
Lift left leg and right arm.
Lift right arm and right leg.
Lift as above but with the arms and/or legs bent, and stretch them in the air.

Find four or five different positions, and repeat them from the beginning to the end, in reverse order or in any other combination. In this section students can choose any position they like – lying on the side, on the stomach, rolling around.

Standing up   Place legs in an open (second) position, arms far apart.
Stretch the arms alternately.
Lift the right leg off the floor, stretch the leg with a flexed foot and the left arm upwards.
Lift one leg and one arm and stretch into various directions around the circle.
Lift one leg and the opposite arm and tilt the body from the pelvis in different directions, at first according to teacher's directions, later according to free choice.
Bend and stretch the lifted leg in the air, as high as possible, according to the students' ability, working on balancing in as many ways and directions as possible – this exercise combines development of sense of shape and sense of balance with the help of an outside factor, making for elongation of the spine (pay attention to free neck and free breathing).
Fix about five positions, starting on the floor, rise to standing position and combine them into a phrase, repeating several times.
Work in couples: using all the elements explored, possibly in mirror vision or any other relationship, paying attention to linear or cubic shapes.
Variations are possible with the use of rostra, chairs, screens and other objects.
All these movements are aesthetically pleasing and physically quite demanding. Well done they should be able to incorporate the principle of reversibility, that is one should be able to start, stop and re-start moving at any given point in the movement without holding the breath.
Now use the four limbs freely from any chosen position, either lying or standing, to create shapes in space according to personal choice, paying attention to the rhythmic quality of the movements.

67

Make a loop from a piece of elastic about 10 yards long and let all the members of the group hold on to it. Start in a circle, work in relationship to one another, stretching and giving alternately.

Alter the basic shape of the circle into a square.

Alter the basic shape of the square into a triangle and other shapes.

Work for variations in height.

Work with background sounds, either change position or movement with every sound, or use more complex rhythms. (A gong is a very effective instrument to use, as well as bells or drums).

Work with composed music as background.

Dramatic themes:

Use the band as a kind of fence, one or two people wanting to escape and the group holding them back.

The group is fenced off, someone wants to intrude from outside; this needs a great deal of working with strength.

Compositions are then prepared by students on their own after the lesson. Our students were asked to use one length of elastic for anything they wanted to do after the experiments in the classroom.

Themes developed were:

A walking triangle

An individual seesaw, then developed into a double seesaw

Open Sesame

The walking snake

The escapologist

The musical door.

Eventually the individual compositions were used as a starting point for work in twos and threes to create fascinating interlocking patterns.

Work with a rope

We help to stir the imagination with a simple object that is extremely flexible. It can work almost like a doodle, expressing a persons unconscious feeling for forms and rhythms.

We use ropes of approximately 100″ length (2.50m).

68

Every member of the group takes a rope and tries to express its flexibility and flow in various shapes.

Divide the group into smaller units of three to five people. One member of the group throws the rope on the floor in any shape he wishes; each member of the group tries to recreate the shape with his own body. The various groups eventually watch each other and talk about their experience and exchange reactions.

Variations   One person throws the rope on the floor and the whole group is asked to recreate the shape in two different versions, once on the floor and once in an upright position.

One person throws the rope, the whole group watches for a short time, then everyone recreates the shape with closed eyes.

The same procedure, then recreate the shape with one leg only.

The same with arms only.

The same with the body and the legs without using the arms.

Work in couples: one person is passive, lying on the

69

floor with eyes closed; the other recreates the shape with his passive body, paying attention not only to the shape itself but also to the quality of the movement which should flow easily.

Imagined Shapes and Qualities of Materials
This kind of work is best preceded by a number of stretching movements (suggested previously) which will serve as a warm-up, and at the same time alert the senses to an awareness of shape, which in this case will act as a neutral starting point for the things to come.

Let the students imagine that they are sheets of *metal*; ask them to move as such, bending in a way that would simulate a metallic quality.

Then let students imagine that they are *silk* or *velvet*; let them move in an appropriate way.

Let students imagine that they are pieces of *paper*; again moving accordingly.

Then let them close their eyes, and ask them to produce equivalent sounds.

Finally go back to the previous movement themes and combine sound and movement.

When all these have been mastered, start changing over from one material to the other – at first slowly, then quickly, then producing the change by touching each other, then by touching the floor in transition from one quality to the next.

After the initial experiments, divide the group into three groups, each representing one material; and start working as an orchestra, calling one member of the group to serve as conductor.

Now you can start creating objects made of these materials, first as individuals then larger objects consisting of two to three people and more. Later on the whole group may combine into forming one large object. We had objects made like

a piece of jewellery worn by a person
a book
fabulous dresses
machines
instruments made of two different materials
pieces of sculpture
rolls of toilet paper
curtains
complicated pieces of antique furniture.

71

While working in this way we have always paid great attention to the way in which people change from being one kind of material to being another. Rhythmical qualities have to be in keeping with the type of material they assume. When we ask the students to change from one to the other by way of touching the floor – using differences in height – the flow of the movement has to be continued. We try to continue to apply the principles of coordination and reversibility of movement, in other words, not to lose alertness to sensory perception. We want to make the body follow our intentions, not to let things 'happen' in the negative sense.

Eventually a group has to work out its own 'story-line'.

Everyone participating in this kind of work finds it imaginatively stimulating; and it also makes for interesting ways of communication between members of the group.

PROJECTS

Sizzling egg in a frying pan
The idea of a frying pan came up in a group working on the idea of metal and its associations, and we decided to turn it into a group choreography.

We started with everyone imitating in movement the frying and sizzling in the pan. Each person was a frying pan. Then one person was eating an egg, another washing the dishes. Someone became Mother feeding baby. This led us to the digestive process. But eventually we came to a dead end. Students said it was boring and that there was no way out. But we did not want to give in. We pointed out to the group that it was very important not to give in, but find a solution to the theme.

After several more experiments lasting over a few weeks the final result was a very charming group experiment. One person broke an egg, composed of eight members of the group, into a frying pan. The students spread out in a circle, feet to the centre, and were at first frying, then sizzling, and were turned over by the 'cook'.
, The cook turned into a man swallowing pieces of egg – these went through his arms, and became the intestines, which began to move slowly, digesting the food. The food turned into the bloodstream, the bloodstream became the womb and out of the womb came a baby that was born with a loud cry.

The Velveteen Rabbit

Another group enacted Margery Williams' story of a rabbit made of cheap velveteen that had to compete with more expensive toys made of metal and wood. Eventually it became the only toy that a sick child wanted in bed. But when the child recovered from scarlet fever the rabbit was thrown away. Eventually the rabbit was turned into a real rabbit by the 'nursery magic Fairy'.

Imagined colours

Patterns of work
The verbal imagery of colours can be used to evoke associations, and develop imaginative work.

Suggested warm-up is work on head and neck and eye movements, rotation on torso.

Colours are suggested by the tutor. Students react to a named colour in word associations and movement, or in abstract sound and frozen movement. The same colour is repeated several times so as to allow for variation in responses.

73

From our own students' collection of images:

Brown – Earth, filth, animals, fascist, monk.

White – Purity, bride, church, nuns, snow, virgin, sheet.

Purple – Majestic, curtain, nothing, flowers, disgust.

Black – Sorrow, night, darkness, monk, depression.

Red – Flag, blood, wounded, fire, violence, bricks, aggression.

Khaki – Army, Germany, boy scouts.

Green – Meadow, vegetable, tree.

Blue – Horizon, sea, scar.

Yellow – Heat, light, sun, desert, thistle, happiness, gaiety, warmth, buttercups, flower.

Orange – Toast, fire (more than red), sweat.

After the initial stages develop a story from the images:

White – Ku Klux Klan, sheet, virgin, clouds, nun.

Red – Bricks, violence, blood, passion, wounded.

Yellow – Buttercups, sunshine, desert, thistle.

Imagined objects

Patterns of work   The procedure is similar to that used in the work with colour.

74

An object is suggested by the tutor; the group reacts to it in pure movement, then in movement and sound, then with verbal associations evoked by the suggested object:

Chair, door, window, ceiling.

House, room (bathroom, kitchen, bedroom).

Cottage, castle, stairs.

Clothes, hats, shoes, bags, scarves.

Tools, hammer, bolts, nuts.

After working like this on individual reactions you can create a common theme, such as 'a room': one person after another joins in to create the room, everyone freezes in one position, naming the object he creates and if he needs to continues with an appropriate noise (like the ticking of a clock or noises from a TV set).

Next suggest variations on the theme: the same room in the early morning hours, five minutes before going to work, after a party, during a game, a quarrel.

You can go on then to groups of themes like scenes from a fairy tale, scenes from everyday life, family events, newspaper reports, in a library, in a swimming pool.

This work is aimed to develop heightened levels of perception of everyday occurrences and observation of details in our surroundings. And it also arouses a very lively sense of group participation.

Discovery of geometrical shapes

Patterns of work Start with a preparation which makes for physiologically sound movement and leads at the same time to a precise awareness of shape.

Stand in a neutral position. Stretch the arms with flexed hands (this relationship between arms and hands is maintained throughout the following movements according to individual ability, the ideal being 90°, that is a right angle). Move the arms at the side plane (2) and (6) along 180° until the hands face the ceiling – the arms move at ear level. From this position release the arms by 45° and return to the high position.

Repeat the same, lowering the arms by 90°, 135°, 180° and continue without stopping, according to ability. Stop in between whenever necessary (so that the arms do not become over-tense), change speeds or accents in rhythm, so that the movement does not become mechanical; release in between each movement for a short rest pause. There is no point in tiring the muscles unnecessarily, as they will tense more than is useful.

Repeat the same movement with the legs, moving with feet flexed, but obviously movements will have a much smaller radius. Adapt the given movement sequence to the students' ability (which will of course vary considerably between, say, art students and professional dancers); start by using the forward plane (0) first, then move into different directions, trying each direction for its particular ability and feeling. Pay great attention to the correct posture throughout, elongation along the spine, freedom of head and neck.

Now start combining arm and leg movements in various combinations – this leads to innumerable possibilities and variations.

At a more advanced stage you can use different timing for the legs and arms.

It is useful at this point to incorporate head movements to achieve different accents, expressions and co-ordinated movements. We shall enlarge upon these in a separate chapter.

After having used the arms thus as one unit you can proceed to create free shapes with them.

Students create imaginary spaces around them and imagine that they are moving inside a sphere, inside a tent, inside a square-shaped room. For differences in size and texture they can move inside prison walls, inside a forest, inside a bus, a train or a boat.

Experiment with a group

One of our groups consisted of first-year drama students, second- and third-year architecture students, and a few sculpture and fine art students.

We let people move in space creating as a group different geometrical shapes, e.g. a square, a triangle, a circle. We tried it with musical accompaniment and without; sometimes the people created the rhythms either with their feet or by clapping hands. Sounds made with the mouth and words were used as rhythms.

We talked about people's reactions, which differed

according to their temperaments. Some found the circle too free, the square more secure, the triangle suggesting a strong drive, while some enjoyed the freedom in a circle.

We concluded that the human factor is all-decisive in personal reactions to space, and that there are no hard and fast rules to be made. One of our colleagues remarked on seeing an end-of-term performance: 'How they reveal themselves!'

Another experiment with a group

We divided a group of seven into one of three and another of four people. The group of four created a square and had to remain in that same relationship, being able to change the size of the shape only; while the group of three created a triangle – they too had to remain in the triangular relationship, though they were allowed to change the size and type of the triangle.

The group creating the triangle proved to be infinitely more interesting than the one moving in a square, in spite of the fact that the latter used much more space and constantly changed the rhythm and size of the square.

The participants agreed that the triangle was by nature the more dynamic shape, for they found absolutely no limitation to the group relationships possible within the form.

The students moving in the square on the other hand found it to be very rigid and limiting.

We then mixed the partners and after another member of the group had arrived, we divided the group into two units of four each.

Through switching the partners we tried to work with different personalities; and this time again one group moved the square around the room, jumping and using as much space as possible, exerting as much energy as possible, working hard physically but looking dull.

The second group chose to remain stationary and work within one definite square – they discovered an almost infinite number of different postures, relationships and movements in this limited space and

77

were very exciting to watch.

When we summed up the experiment, the first group expressed boredom, said they felt limited, uninspired and dull; whereas the second group found it 'fantastic', exciting and interesting and said they did not know that one could do so many different things with a mere square.

Once more the human factor is all-decisive; the second group had worked with the greater degree of concentration and better human relationships, better and more creative contact, and a more mature approach. So they had gained in experience in a way that the first group had not.

Emotional experience expressed in movement terms

We suggested to first-year drama students that they write down five things that made them angry, happy or sad, and five things of their own choice.

The following were among the answers we received:

Things to make us *angry* were – intolerance, pollution, red tape, injustice, waiting, rudeness, yobbos, drivers not indicating in good time, needless violence, people not reading books, the system of mental homes, litter-dropping, apathy, people who let you down, inefficiency, especially here!!!, people telling me I have an inferiority complex when actually they have a superiority complex, spite, deceit, authority when misused, narrow mindedness, President Nixon, the power of teachers, drunken teenage girls.

Things to make us *happy* were – sun, music, my car 'Belinda' (when she goes), colour pink, giving presents, receiving affection, people caring for each other, the spontaneous side of life, books, creating things, happy children, having a lie in bed, mountains, dancing, affection, flowers, friends, food, pulling faces, being in command of what I'm doing, being silly in public places, doing mad things just because I feel like doing it, fast driving when it's safe, being in love.

Things to make us *sad* were – bigotry and prejudice, vested interests, e.g. when B.P. bought rights on electric car and scrapped it, cruelty to children, A.B.

(Head of Dept.), C.D. (the Head of School), rain, arguments, getting up in the morning, death, usually sad after being angry or hurting people, people who are late and never turn up, seeing little grubby neglected kids ask for money in the streets, frustration, poverty of others, my father, people who don't trust one another, people who can't see further than their own noses, big concrete cities, wars, inmates of mental institutions, being lonely, music.

Other qualities suggested included *Silly* things – getting lost in a city I have lived in for 14 years, a bit of my car falling off as I drive along.

Scary things – bees, wasps.

Frightening things – thunderstorms (but I enjoy them really), rats, guns, warfare, being alone too much, anything athletic, the dentist, exposing myself to criticism.

Uncomfortable things – glare, noise, 'cobwebs in the brain'.

We asked the students to select any of their chosen subjects to make a movement composition from. Eventually we presented a programme at the end of term consisting of a choice of students' own work bearing the following titles:

Don't shoot me I'm Elton John
Weather Woman
Sad-happy feet
What shall we do now?
Sea – Thunder – Lightning
City-Phobia
Inflicting pain and enjoying it
Failed Escapologist
Diana Ross sings Bessie Smith
Little boy playing by himself
It
A way out
Disillusion
Whereabouts
Shanti Lion Wobble
The greatest discovery since sliced wheels
H – B (which represented in a grotesque manner fear of nuclear war)

Develop characters

Choose an object to sit on: a chair, a bench, box or rostrum. Use it in an obvious way, then use it in an unusual way (to become a rocking chair, an easy chair, a swing, a seesaw or a rocking-horse).

Accent each time the way of sitting down and getting up – in a correct way and then in the way an invented character would do it, stressing his idiosyncracies.

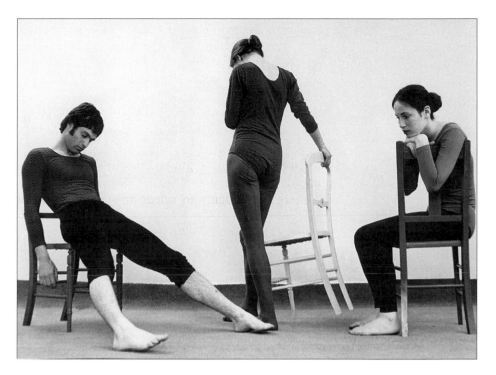

Work on different age groups: children, young
people, grown ups and old people. Make the different
characters of each age group sit down in a manner that
is:
      patient – impatient
      nervous – easygoing
      happy – melancholic
      serious – flippant.
  Work on different imaginary locations:
      public park
      restaurant
      seaside
      balconies in a city
      railway
      a football match
      theatre or concert audience
      waiting rooms – government or consular office –
      wartime – peacetime – doctor's waiting room, audi-
      tioning
      church, synagogue or other place of worship.

Work on sharp and quick transitions from one character to another; Depict the same character at different
times of his life, changing quickly from one period to the
next, changing from one location to another:
    at the seaside – the same person as a boy and old man
    – a bench in a public park – sitting there as a young
    person – growing old gradually.
Divide the whole group into various locations, and
into people of different ages.
    Pay special attention to:
    use of various parts of the body – feet, knees, pelvis,
    torso, the relationship of head and neck; arms, shoul-
    ders, hands, face; the feeling of the skin, the feel of the
    muscles, the weight of the bones; the use of clothing,
    shoes, trousers, dresses, hats, gloves, umbrella, walk-
    ing stick.

The story of a poem
We asked the students to prepare in their holidays a
composition based on a poem. One of the most intrigu-
ing creations was that of a girl who chose 'All there is to
know about Adolph Eichmann' by Leonard Cohen.

She entered like a clown turning cartwheels, then stood in front of us speaking and illustrating the text:

Eyes – medium
Hair – medium
Weight – medium
Height – medium
Distinguishing features – none
Number of fingers – ten
Number of toes – ten
Intelligence – medium
What did you expect?

She then went off stage and entered again, turning cartwheels.

What did you expect?
Talons?
Oversize incisors?
Green saliva?
Madness?

With the last word she burst into a loud cry.

This was done very effectively – counterpointing in a grotesque fashion the movements with the factual statement of the poem, that read like the bald text of any file. What really do files express, seemed to be the meaning, how much do they contain of the person's life?

We all felt that this poem is worth exploring in the group.

We started to improvise. At first we suggested a busy street with people using the text of the poem (the group numbered nine members), but this did not lead to any follow-up. We then started using chairs, everyone using a chair in his or her own way, climbing up, calling out to another, climbing down, walking around the chair. This looked more promising and in the following classes we explored the medium further.

Here are some of the notes we took in the first improvisations, thinking that eventually we might choreograph the whole scene from these beginnings:

3 chairs in a row,

Amanda running through,

Christine jumping over chair,

one word repeated by the whole group,

conversation – two people around one chair,

Peter standing on the ladder – saying 'madness' repetitively,

Stephanie turn on ten,

a row of chairs representing a railway.

All this appeared promising but it eventually disappeared with repetition.

We then started by chanting 'medium' 'medium' 'medium' in a long humming sound which eventually became our opening tone. This was sung while everyone was almost stationary on or around his/her chair. Then we experimented with variations of words until finally everyone had three words to repeat in various intonations and in the order he/she wanted, so that we eventually created an orchestrated sound-and-movement poem. We worked at the time in what we called 'Colditz', our vast, dark, cold and noisy auditorium. The whole scene became a haunting experience, each student creating a melody from his/her words, two members of the group using the railway made from a few chairs, and all eventually ending on one heap with just a few arms sticking out.

5 Structure of a Lesson

If it is your wish, my son,
>you can be trained;
>if you give your mind to it,
>you can become clever;
>if you enjoy listening,
>you will learn

Ecclesiasticus 6, 32

In the following pages a number of structured lessons are presented, each one concerning a single subject that can be presented in one single lesson.

SOUND AND MOVEMENT
This lesson is intended to:
a. develop a sense of rhythm
b. prepare children and actors to make their own musical instruments
c. integrate a new group coming together for the first time.

To warm up

1 Ask students to respond to a *given* rhythm:
   a. walking around in space
   b. running around in space
   c. combining walking and running alternately.

Then ask students to use their *own* rhythm:
a. walking and running alternately
b. walking, running and stopping alternately
c. walking, running and stopping – then changing the level of the body to low and high
d. walking, running and stopping, lowering their bodies, then proceeding on the floor and returning to the beginning of the phrase.

All the above elements can be used in any sequence chosen, so that not everybody will move at the same time in the same way. It is the student's own responsibility to decide the order of events, the direction, the timing and the continuation of each element, in his/her own personal phrase, which is to be repeated at least three times.

The foot – different contacts with the floor	2 Ask students to explore different parts of the foot by touching the floor in various ways:

    a. with the ball of the foot only
    b. with the heel only
    c. alternately with ball and heel.

Ask students to sense the floor:
    a. shift the weight of the body around the sole of the foot in a circular motion clockwise
    b. repeat (a) anticlockwise
    c. repeat (a) and (b) alternately.

Changing relationship of leg to floor:
    a. touch the floor with the ball of the foot in different directions in space – close to or away from each other.
    b. repeat (a) with open or closed hip joints.

Movement and sound added

3 Making sounds:
    a. touch the floor beating as wide a range of rhythms as possible, using the floor like a drum.
    b. everyone is asked to create a phrase of his/her own, containing elements of the sounds and movements just explored – to be repeated at least three times.

Work in couples

4 Creative development:
    a. 'Questions and answers' – a conversation with feet.
    b. 'Echo-game' – one partner starts to beat a phrase – the partner repeats it like an echo.

Work in groups

5 Work in two groups instead of couples: decide on a leader for each group, like a tribal leader, and create:
    a. a conversation between two leaders and their groups
    b. a group version of the 'Echo-game'.

The hands: different contacts with either floor or body

6 Produce sounds with different parts of the hands: the palms, the back of the hands, the nails, the fingers. Play with as many sounds as possible
    a. on the floor
    b. on the body, then

c. single members of the group stand up to demonstrate the phrases they have created, and the group follows.

7 Integrate into a personal phrase a combination of foot and hand movement-sounds.

Summing up

At last the whole group is distributed around the studio to form an orchestra containing all elements used so far. This is conducted by one member of the group.

DEVELOPMENT OF SITTING POSITIONS

This lesson aims to develop:
  a. use of floor and space
  b. variety in use of the body
  c. memory of direction.

Patterns of work

Ask students to sit crossed-legged – oriental position. To the sound of a gong or any other continuous sound (triangle, bells etc.) change to another position. Try many different ways of sitting, every time with the sound.

Find five definite sitting positions.

Change from one position to another (4 transitions) in the following ways:
  in the shortest possible way; slow and fast;
  in the longest possible way; slow and fast;
  by way of rolling over the floor;
  by touching the floor with as many parts of the body as possible: abdomen, back, pelvis, hands;
  by changing the height, such as by standing on knees, standing on soles of feet.

Every person makes a movement phrase consisting of four or five fixed positions in the same order, using a different transition from each position, eventually being able to repeat the phrase many times.

Variation: everyone works his sequence in reverse.

Choral
movement

Divide a group according to size into smaller groups of three to five people each.

The leader of a group conducts it like an orchestra: each group has *one definite way of moving* from one position to another – the conductor determines the order and the number of groups working at any one time.

92

The following was presented to one of our classes as one drama student's homework in the second week of the first term.

Exercise: to find five ways of sitting down to be carried out at three speeds:
    a. normal tempo
    b. slow motion
    c. accelerated to double speed.

Here is one of several sequences performed:
  I standing position cross legs, lower body into crossed legged sitting position
  II arms back supporting weight, legs wide extended in front in open position
  III knees drawn up to chest, straight back
  IV lean back on elbows, one knee bent upwards other leg lying at right angles to it on the ground
  V reclining position lying on one side of the body.

Ideas for developing sequences:
1 Two people work together so that one mirrors the movements of the other.
2 Do the movements in a round, i.e. one person starts first movement, and as he finishes and procceds into second movement, the next person begins first movement etc. (wavelike motion).
3 One movement is performed by different people in sequence one after the other.
4 Two people working simultaneously show contrasts between open and closed movements.
5 Perform sequences in varying rhythms, maybe staccato, legato, etc.
6 Accompany movements with appropriate sounds.
7 Adopt characters and perform accordingly.
8 Perform sequences puppet-fashion, or like a clockwork toy losing speed.

INSECTS AND ANIMALS – CONTRACTION AND RELEASE OF THE EXTREMITIES
When we had to produce Carel Capek's play *The Insect World*, we wanted to achieve the best possible realism.

So we set out
a. to observe the insect in nature
b. to achieve control over the limbs without tension, and with utmost freedom of the joints
c. to effect personal transformation through precise awareness of the body.

So we evolved the following exercises:
Ask students to

Standing
a. Stretch the arms while standing on a spot. Legs are parallel, hands are fisted, stretch the arms in different directions, using them mainly in an asymmetrical way to achieve maximum expansion. The head may be used to produce yawning movements, the stretching should be animal-fashion.
b. Next move closer to the floor, bending so that the body can be parallel to the floor, hands opening. Continue stretching to maximum extension away from the centre.
c. Then kneel on the floor while stretching the arms and torso with open stretched fingers.

Lying
d. Lying on the floor contract and release alternately the following: toes first without moving anything else, fingers without moving anything else, toes and fingers without moving anything else. Flex the ankles and contract toes simultaneously, release; flex wrist and contract fingers simultaneously, release. Flex ankles and wrists and contract toes and fingers simultaneously, release.
e. Contract the lower leg – this is possible only by turning on the side or the abdomen – release; contract lower leg, ankle and toes simultaneously, release; contract the lower arm only, release; contract lower arm, wrist and fingers simultaneously, release; contract lower leg, lower arm, wrists, ankles, toes and fingers simultaneously, release.
f. Return to lying on the back, stretch the arms above the head, legs straight – pull the right leg up to vertical position (or more) – release; pull up right leg and right arm to vertical parallel line; release; repeat with the left side. Pull up right leg and left arm, release;

repeat with left leg and right arm, release; pull up both legs and arms to vertical.

g. From this position bend and stretch arms and legs into different directions: symmetrically, parallel, in various directions, every limb into a different direction.

Students' comments	'I feel like a frog' 'Do we practise becoming tortoises?' 'Feels like an insect' 'It is very pleasant to do'.
Variation	h. Students are encouraged to shift the weight on to different parts of the back while experimenting with all the preceding variations.
On four limbs	i. Shifting the weight on to hands and feet, move around in space forward, backward, sideways, using the limbs either symmetrically or parallel.
Individual improvisation	Students can choose any inspiration from the insect world: flies, bees, spiders, beetles. Find one or two other people in the group to communicate with.

95

Homework	1 Go outside into a garden, park, forest or zoo to observe animals and insects in natural surroundings. 2 Create an insect either as an abstract movement composition or a dramatic character.

EMOTIONAL RESPONSE TO SHAPES

Images from the unconscious bring about a stillness, a concentration coming from inner resources. The response of the person to one image at a time develops the imagination.

Ask students to close their eyes and speak aloud their associations – as many as come to their mind as response to:

> a straight line
> a square
> a circle
> a triangle.

If they like they can write their images on paper.

Development	a. Ask the whole group to decide on one of the four subjects. Everyone individually develops one of his own images in movement. b. Small groups are formed, each developing one of the images. All perform together like an orchestra.
From our experience	The following are some of the images we worked with: **a straight line**: speed – a call – a laserbeam – a queue – boulevard – balance – rigidity. **a square**: cage – fence – house – ceiling – door – boredom – confidence – flatness. **a circle**: sunflower – ritual drum – freedom – hula hoop – perpetuum mobile – selfconfidence – 'diabolo'. **a triangle**: arrow – sharpness – ladder – crystal – *No Exit* by Sartre.

THE DRAMATIC MEANING OF ARM MOVEMENTS

To begin with explore the functional movements of hands: palms and back of the hands, wrists, fingers; lower arms, upper arms, shoulders.

This experience leads to a wealth of imaginative interpretations.

Walking Ask students to walk in the studio. They meet each other, and
a. touch one person with palms only, repeat several times;

b. touch each other on meeting with the lower arm only;

c. touch each other on meeting with the upper arm only;

d. meet (still one person only) with one of the parts mentioned, but add a change of height and speed. Change partners after every touch.

e. After these movements become easy and flowing, do the same again but this time touch two people at a time, not necessarily with the same part of the arm, so that one may meet two people, touching one person with the hand, the other with the lower arm etc.

Sitting

Sit down on the floor in an oriental position, legs crossed over. Now everyone works by himself.

a. Palms are held touching each other in front of the chest: move the arms in this fixed position in every direction possible, allowing the shoulders and elbows to stretch and bend as necessary.

b. Fix the wrists together, let the fingers move as much as possible, while the wrists remain in loose contact.

c. Work now with each hand separately: clench the fingers to form a fist, at first straight, then letting the arms participate, close to the body and away from the body, continue opening and closing the hand.

Combination

d. Vary the dynamics of the movement, starting with strong and staccato movements, short and long, then change to soft flowing and legato movements; finally everyone makes his own phrase, like a melody.

Creative interpretation

Ideas

a. Using the flexibility of the fingers students are asked to move the fingers to represent human activities according to their own choice:

playing a flute – mending a fisherman's net – shaving – playing the piano – rubbing the eyes – manicuring fingernails – weaving – turning the pages of a book.

b. Continue the finger and hand movements, then on request freeze in action, letting the whole body take the character of the person performing the task.

c. Now students stand up, move the arms as one unit

from the shoulders only, with straight elbows. Use both arms at once to make large and small circles, working only parallel; then using both arms to chase each other. Every movement starts slowly, increasing speed as much as possible.

Ideas

Using all joints of the arm, swim in different ways, paddle a canoe, row a boat, put things high up on a cupboard; hang out sheets.

d. At last arms are used bent, so that the accent is turned to the elbows. Start by forming a queue in which a number of people try to push their way to the front. Then stand on one spot, arms bent, bringing the elbows close to the body and far from the body, make circles, turn to more aggressive movements, pushing the neighbour, or stretching a tight garment.

Ideas in couples

This leads to work in couples:
    fighting each other;
    molesting each other,
    flirting with each other.

Finally form an orchestra, one person conducting; then form two orchestras, one playing pop music, one classical music.

WORK WITH AN OBJECT

The chair – not only to sit on. The infinite possibilities inherent in a chair: as a structure or shape with a texture; as something to sit on; as stimulus for associations – how far can imagination stretch?

Warm up

Chairs are spread around the studio.

Students run around the chairs without touching them.

On a given signal: stop without touching a chair; stop, touching the chair in any way possible; stop in a position that is lower than the seat of the chair; stop in a position lower than the seat of the chair, but related to it, like putting an arm or a leg underneath, head underneath or the back underneath; stop in a position relating to a distant chair with a dramatic purpose, such as longing for, admiring, disagreeing with, challenging, being interested in the chair relating from above or beneath.

Working on a chair	Sit on a chair so that the feet won't touch the floor. Change the base to off-balance positions: choose three or four different positions, and make a sequence by moving from one position to the next, and repeat the sequence several times, using varying speeds; make the body as small as possible and as large as possible in different directions and speeds.
Working with the chair	Put the chair on the floor in any possible way. Move the body relating to the shape that appears, for example crawl underneath, step over, balance with the chair, changing the position of the chair each time.
Ideas	The chair then becomes any object.

Our students suggested that the chair become
    a prison,
    a baby's playpen,
    a chariot,
    a fisherman's boat,
    a saucepan.
Once an object has been chosen, relate to it:
    as a young person,

a middle-aged person,
an old person.
Let the chair become an extension of the personality:
the person's idea,
problem,
infatuation,
fate,
faith,
curiosity,
sense of humour,
surprise,
vanity,
love.

It is amazing how many different identities one simple object can take on, and how many transformations it will lend itself to.

Among the reactions and comments we have had from our students are the following:

'I found as the exercise developed I developed a close relationship with the chair. It became a stronger image of my personality and I was able to use it in a more interesting and varied way.'

'Initially I found we had to choose between being symbolistic in our attitude to the subject, or use the chair to express the reality of it.'

'. . . however when we started transforming the chair into our extensions it became for me something of which I was very aware, something upon which I was totally dependent. When the chair was "your ideal" I didn't take much notice of the physical aspect of the chair . . .'

'. . . it had become something very personal to me, something I was at once affectionate to and scared of, I was very attached to it and hated to leave it behind.'

'. . . As the exercise wore on I found myself less and less violent towards the chair. However I could not show complete passion for a chair . . . the more the exercise wore on again the more I began to respect the chair as a non-chair . . . through this you could profess dignity, charm, elegance, or use it as a

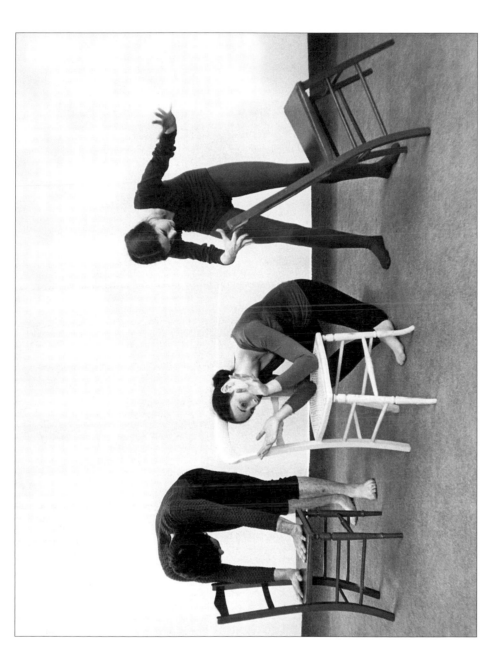

weapon . . . a definite relationship was growing . . . in a sense it gave you a release, a key to relieve tension or inspiration, which perhaps you would keep inside you . . .'

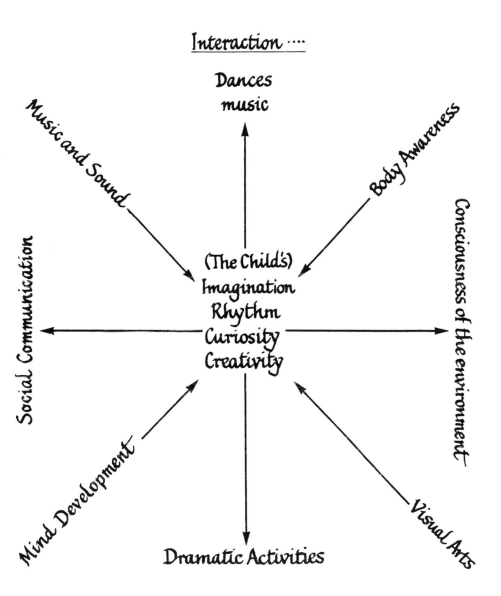

Interaction ....

Dances
music

Music and Sound

Body Awareness

Social Communication

Consciousness of the environment

(The Child's)
Imagination
Rhythm
Curiosity
Creativity

Mind Development

Visual Arts

Dramatic Activities

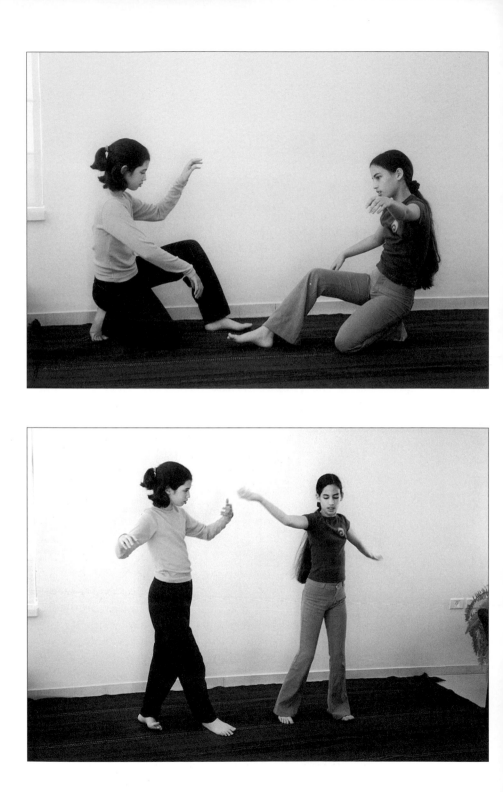

6 Work with Children Age Four to Twelve

All arts are siblings
kindling one another,
jointly giving everlasting glow

Voltaire

The imagination is the most powerful drive in a child's life and so we need to create an atmosphere in which children can give expression to their hidden inner world.

A child's imaginative world is nourished on feelings and impressions; a child wants to identify with fairy-tale heroes, with animals it adores and is afraid of, such as snakes, dogs and wolves, to become just for a short while a king, a princess or a dancer.

Children need to express their dreams as well as their fears. Their imaginative world expressed through movement leaves a memory much livelier and more colourful than purely verbal, visual or audible experience.

We take great care not to suppress the child's inner drive, but to create the atmosphere and the right attitude for the child to feel secure, and to present material to him (her) in a way in which he will want to create; not dominating and giving orders, but steadily pointing out new directions in which to work.

Free expression within a given frame enriches the experience and enlarges the horizon of a child. At this point it is worth mentioning that often the teacher can learn from the children, and certainly the children learn from each other. The unexpected visitor to classes taught in this way will find himself in the middle of an exciting piece of choreographed movement. The concentration achieved by this brings self-discipline and co-operation, give and take, creative coexistence, orientation in space, kinaesthetic awareness (learning not to interfere with each other, to be tolerant and patient).

In our work children become aware of and know the body, its different parts and its mobility from age four onwards. They acquire this knowledge and ability by experiencing and discovering the body in activities

109

designed for this purpose. The movement lessons run parallel to children's work in the classroom and in close co-operation with their teacher.

Every theme and project covered in the classroom is being reintroduced through the body and the imagination, enlarging the understanding of the child and his ability to communicate with his surroundings.

Some themes worked with are:
      Numbers
      The Weather
      Fire
      Transport-Vehicles.
Work with materials includes:
      Paperbags
      Rugs or Sheets
      Clothes and props
      Percussion Instruments

PROJECTS

Project – numbers

From our experience we have learned how useful the following work is for young children, increasing their awareness of the flow, direction and shape of numbers, helping them in the art of learning to read and to write. This is always done parallel to work in class and in close co-operation with their general teacher.

We approach numbers in three different ways: walking the pattern on the floor; drawing the shapes in the air with different parts of the body; being a number, like a sculpture.

All numbers consist of lines and circles, so we start by walking in straight lines, in circular lines and in lines that meet at an angle, like the numbers 4 or 7: two children make a number 7, each walking half the shape; each child by himself walks a 0; each child walks an 8. Now we take the combinations of lines and curves, like a 2 or a 5, and ask them to find out for themselves what numbers can be made from a line and a circle.

Children stand on a spot and draw the numbers in the air with one arm, large and small, imagining that their

111

arm is a pencil; we ask the children to write numbers with different parts of the arm (hands, fingers, elbow).

Now they are asked to draw the imaginary numbers with any part of their body they can think of: head, torso, legs or feet. When this is done they can work on balance beautifully.

At last they are becoming the number, making the whole body into the desired shape like a piece of sculpture, like 2 which can be done standing on their knees; or 8 which gives rich curves to the whole body. The numbers can be suggested in various ways: the teacher can draw the number in the air in front of the children; or the teacher can indicate by giving a beat which children have to interpret or by just saying the number.

When children have some idea of the shapes of the numbers we start playing games; accent on quantity – children work in couples making decimal numbers like 23, 57 etc. Some children make the numbers and the other children have to guess; children make up questions like 8 + 1 ?, 5 + 12 ?, and the answer has to be made in movement; large groups make up questions like 47 + 25? Divide into groups, ask a certain number of children to come forward at a given sign – 1, 2, 3, 4 children at a time – then go back to their groups; adding and subtracting. Stand 10 children in a row, and to a given sign one child at a time bends or stretches; children make their own numbers, calling out 3, 5, 7 etc.; the rest have to form into groups of that denomination.

Suggest numbers to the children and let them choose the type of movement by which they want to show the number, such as by making large steps, small steps, jumping, skipping or just being a sculpture standing or lying.

The same approach can be used with regard to letter-writing in the beginning of their lessons. Letters will be made up into various words, or children can write their name, or write a word to each other, then become the word, either in shape or feeling.

Project – weather
The project on weather gives the children the impulse to look outside the classroom at nature, smell the air, feel

the temperature, be aware of seasonal changes and the power of natural forces.

Wind   How does it blow? Fast – slowly – gently – strongly; walk and run in these different ways; make the sound the wind makes as it blows in different ways; be an object being blown by the wind; work in couples – one child being the wind, the other the object being blown; ask the children about different objects being blown, such as leaves, paper, hats, scarves, treetops, field of wheat or corn, flowers, or the more abstract clouds; be the shapes of clouds, the shapes can then be changed by the wind.

Cloud Make groups of clouds; several children can make different types of clouds – we use a gong to accompany the changes.

All this can be made an introduction to the seasons, beginning with autumn:

In *autumn* ask children to bring in many different leaves from outside – look at the shape of the leaves and the colour, the dryness, then be the shapes of the leaves, and the shapes of the trees from which the leaves came.

Work on the movement qualities, the falling and flying of the leaves, their rolling on the earth, their various speeds using what has been discovered before about the wind; relate the general experience of working on clouds to the special clouds appearing in autumn.

In *winter*, ask what is the special quality of the season? Most will say the cold, so we work on feeling cold, wearing warm clothes, using contractions and releases in different parts of the body, shrinking and expanding, developing physical awareness. Then imagine: rain – light rain – heavy rain – make the sound of rain using the body as a percussive instrument; people and animals hiding from the rain, running in the rain, jumping over puddles, walking in the mud; walking with an umbrella and boots in rain and wind; lightning and thunder; make the shape of lightning, the sound of thunder; rain and snow; different qualities of rain and snow, snowflakes; build a snowman and let it melt away.

In *spring* we ask what is new? Children will say that

114

flowers bud, trees awaken and new leaves grow, the air is fresh, the sun shines, the wind is light, the clouds are light. Practise: growing from small to large using deep and high dimensions; butterflies and birds flying; the flow of movement, particularly in the torso, which can be interpreted as trees growing in the upper parts.

A very nice way of working on this theme is to use the story of 'The Giant and his Garden' by Oscar Wilde.

In *summer* children will point out that heat is the most important thing, and that the sun is shining. The sun rises in the east, sets in the west, the sun has rays and great light and warmth; we can expand into desert, sand and thorns; we can make the prickly, staccato movements of the thorns; we can contrast the movement of the expanding rays of the sun with the short sharp movements of the thorns.

A group can be divided into four seasons, each group chosing for themselves how they want to represent it. We can then move the children around according to season; and add musical accompaniment.

Project Fire

We involve children by acting out the specific characteristics of the fire as they observe it in their environment; by physical imaginative creation they enlarge their sense-memory and perception. Through this movement experience we help children to understand and clarify abstract concepts of basic science such as expansion and contraction, solid and fluid states.

The Flame

In sitting position, ask the children to describe a flame with one part of the body only; in sitting position ask the children to describe a flame with one part of one leg only; in sitting position ask the children to describe a flame with two parts of their bodies; in sitting position ask the children to describe a flame with the torso only; in sitting position ask the children to be a flame by starting a movement in one part of the body and spreading it until the whole body becomes involved and the fire spreads out – rhythmically this is a good example of a

115

movement crescendo; now use crescendo and decrescendo, becoming large and small flames using space.

Work in couples   Next, children are asked to make sounds of fire; one child makes the sound, the other moves to it; do the same with percussion instruments; transfer the movement of fire from one part of the body to the partner, who uses another part of the body. All the above movements can be used freely – standing or lying as we choose.

Fire changes the properties of materials
Children are asked to state what kind of materials burn quickly, slowly, what changes shape.

We tried: to be a piece of paper being burnt; a sheet of nylon disappearing quickly; a rope burning, slowly disintegrating; dry thistles burning in a field; wood turning to coal by being burnt; iron melting when heated and changing its shape; tin melting quicker than iron; water turned to gas and evaporating by being boiled; glass melting into liquid, which can then be transformed into a different shape.

So far we have explored: solid state – fluidity – gas; contraction – expansion – combustion.

Work in small groups   Now children divide up the roles they are playing, being in turn the fire, the material, the sound. One group is fire – iron – sculptor; another group is fire – bellows – glass; another a kettle – the water inside – fire burning.

Work with whole group   The whole group becomes one long rope that is gradually consumed by a slow fire.

Musical terms can easily be incorporated in the drama, and so can sounds made by the children, according to the properties of the materials used.

Fire – Man's Friend and Enemy – A Ritual Symbol
Group work   Fire can be used for cooking, heating, lighting. These functions all suggest themes to be dramatised in larger groups.

Students start by emphasizing the feeling of heat and cold: materials contract in cold and expand in heat, so the class works on making the body flexible – developing from the centre to the extremities and vice versa,

116

from the extremities into the centre. Movement suggests frozen bodies being warmed – unfrozen – by heat.

Forest fire – thistle field

From an individual through the whole group

A careless person throws a burning cigarette into the forest on a hot day – slowly a fire spreads through the dried leaves, eventually setting the trees on fire. Apply the same theme to a field of thistles : stress the sounds the fire would make: sometimes the role of fire can be taken over by a drum, sometimes by a child carrying the fire through the group.

A Ritual Symbol

Illustrate early man's discovery of fire: rub two stones together; rub two limbs together.

Take care of the fire.

Pray to the fire.

Work in circles

Explore the ritual content of movement: make repetitive ritual movements; beat a rhythm with hands and feet.

Bass ostinato

The whole group sustains one rhythmic phrase, one child at a time taking turns to lead the group with a new movement.

Transport – Vehicles

Through work on the concept of a wheel children can discover an essential quality of motion and rhythm. Since the wheel is the basis of most means of transport, they become aware of road behaviour and the highway code. An elementary understanding of speed is reached imaginatively.

The opening theme deals with the wheel. The children make circles with different parts of the body, drawing circular shapes of varying sizes: they draw circles with the feet only, while sitting or lying; they draw circles with the lower leg only, sitting or lying; standing, they draw circles with the thighs only, with the torso only, with the head only, with the pelvis only, with the shoulders only, with the lower arm only, with the hands only, with the fingers only; using the whole arm, they draw vertical circles like the wheels of a carriage.

Co-ordination

With one arm following the other, like a bicycle; they work with two different limbs at the same time, such as

117

one arm and one leg; they work with three different limbs at the same time: head, arm and leg; pelvis, head and one arm.

Children choose their own variations, making up phrases of circular movements, one limb following the other; phrases are made up slow-fast, fast-slow and in any variation; two children make up phrases for each other.

Rolling – somersaults – use of the floor
Ask the children to simulate a wheel by using the floor; ask the children to differentiate between small wheels and large wheels. Rolls are basically of two kinds: for-ward–backward, and sideways. There can also be a combination of both.

Let the children work together in couples so they can find rhythms common to each other; make a point of using slow and fast rhythms. Then let children work as teams of four or six to create symmetrical movement and rhythm patterns (like those of a small car or lorry). Finally let children create their own imagined vehicles and invent names for them.

Various types of transport
Transport by sea: accent on off-balance movements, shift of weight; simulate the feeling of being at sea, sway-ing movements; work in teams: canoes, rafts, rowing boats, sailing boats. Next use the rhythms of the motion of a train: coordination of various limbs, and between members of a team; explore rhythms of trains ap-proaching and disappearing – crescendo, decrescendo.

Form groups and make the sounds of vehicles moving at sea, in the air or on rails and road.

Use the signs of the highway code in movements and shapes, to make children aware of road hazards.

Collective Games – work on characters and imagination
Let the children create a bus stop: one child starts and creates the location, the others join accordingly; pay at-tention to creation of a character, make people of differ-ent ages, wearing different clothes, different shoes; in different kinds of weather.

Create a railway station: act many different characters; buying tickets, carrying suitcases, hurrying to catch a train; attendants, porters, and other officials; freeze in positions, unfreeze; make words and sounds, gibberish.

Similar games can be played at airports.

The games can be adapted to different age groups.

WORK WITH MATERIALS

Ask the children to bring paperbags to the studio.

Let everyone put a paperbag over his head, to cover the face.

The task is to walk around without being able to see, listening to the other children; various ways of moving in space can be employed:

walking,
jumping,
sitting down,
getting up,
walking in specified directions,
walking without touching each other,
turning etc.

Use larger paperbags and make them into different hats, to change the personality. Turn into:

a king,
a rabbit,
a cock,
a funny woman,
a tortoise.

Use the largest paperbags available, either to step through or to pull over the head until it rests on shoulders or hips.

Now the paper is able to change the whole body, its movements, character, behaviour. Become: an elephant, a bear, a fish, a snake, a peacock, a fat man, a monk, a clown, a baby, a lady, a ballerina.

The point is to open the children's eyes and minds to look around for simple means to stir the imagination.

Collect a number of light rugs or sheets or any other large pieces of cloth.

Divide the children into small groups of three to five,

and cover each group with one piece of material. Ask the children to move in relationship to each other, so as to: change height – up and down; change width – wide and narrow; combine both height and width; move separate parts of the body – fingertips only, upper arm only, lower arm only, the whole arm, pelvis only, head only, touch each other with toes only (lying down); combine various elements.

When each group has become acquainted with the material and the people, they can start on group activities. One child becomes the leader and asks different groups into action. Every group can have a name, a number or colour.

According to the skill of the leader the groups can be led into various spaces, children can be lifted, fairy-tales can be employed – they can make a white mountain, a black forest, create a well, streams, valleys, freeze into rocks, etc.

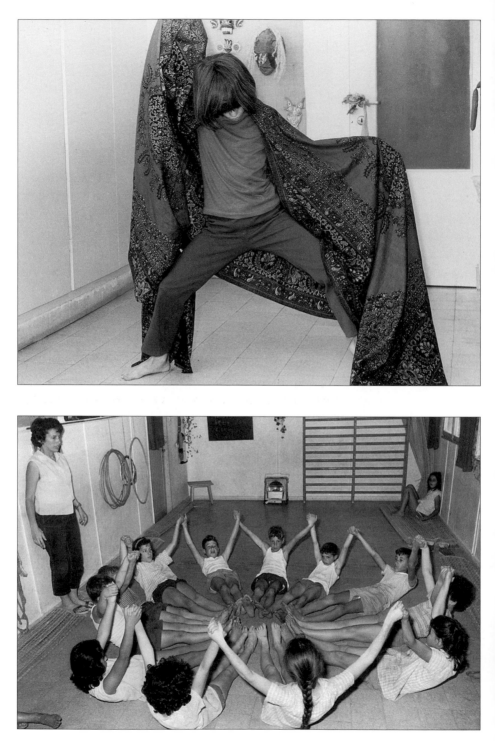

The Use of Clothes, Props, Masks and Percussion Instruments as a stimulus to improvise with children up to age nine.

Integrating the making of masks and creation of character

Children make masks by themselves, either from paper or a variety of materials.

They create the character behind the mask, working at first from a mirror vision, then in couples in contrasting characters. We use legends and parables by La Fontaine, Krilov, Aesopos.

For years we have kept a 'Magic Box' full of costumes, pieces of clothing such as hats, scarves, masks, skirts made of various materials and parts of animal costumes. We also keep a selection of percussion instruments in the studio.

Every child is asked to choose one or two pieces of clothing as a symbol from which to create a character.

a. Each child introduces himself through movement only. A group of five or six children make up a dance-drama.

b. We make up a dramatic story like a 'happening' according to the costumes introduced; anything such as a jungle, a visit to an unknown country, a king's court.
   Children may respond in movement alone or in movement and speech.

c. A mixed event can be created by introducing percussion instruments either to be used as part of their costumes or to accompany their friends.
   Sections a. and b. are mostly accompanied by music.

TATE GALLERY – MOVEMENT, SHAPE AND COLOUR

The Tate Gallery holds a permanent exhibition of sculpture created in the 1960s. These sculptures reflect the positive, materialist, confident style of sculptures from that era; they use bright colours, and free shapes not bound by the human image.

Attached to this the Tate Gallery runs an Educational Project, called 'Movement, Shape and Colour', directed by Terry Measham. We were introduced to this adventure by Nira's 5-year-old son Zivi.

125

Our idea was to acquaint children with modern art, to make visits to museums a joyful experience. We wanted to involve children actively with the sculpture – to make it a live experience.

We wanted:

a. to make them understand what was behind the visual aspect, to learn more about shapes and the qualities of materials;

b. to make them respond spontaneously in individual and group improvisations stimulated by the sculptures;

c. to extend the physical and visual aspects into their own creative outlet in painting and sculpture.

We usually open our session with a promenade – a walk around the sculptures: looking, touching, absorbing and talking about the experience. We ask the children to name the sculptures. Here are some of their names:

	original name	renamed by children
Tim Scott	Quinquereme	Windmill, Aeroplane, Piece of Cake
William Turnbull	5 × 1	Forest, Prison, Traffic Jam
Michael Bolus	4th Sculpture	Roofs, Rocks, Flying Hats
Isaac Witkin	Alter Ego	Paddle, Sandclock
William Tucker	Meru I	Staircase, Gate, Papercut
Neville Boden	Blow in the Ear	Folded Paper, Shell
Phillip King	Dunstable Reel	Bow and Arrow, Crown, Sailing Boat
David Annesley	Jump	Letter M, Snake, Arch, Gate, Optical Glasses

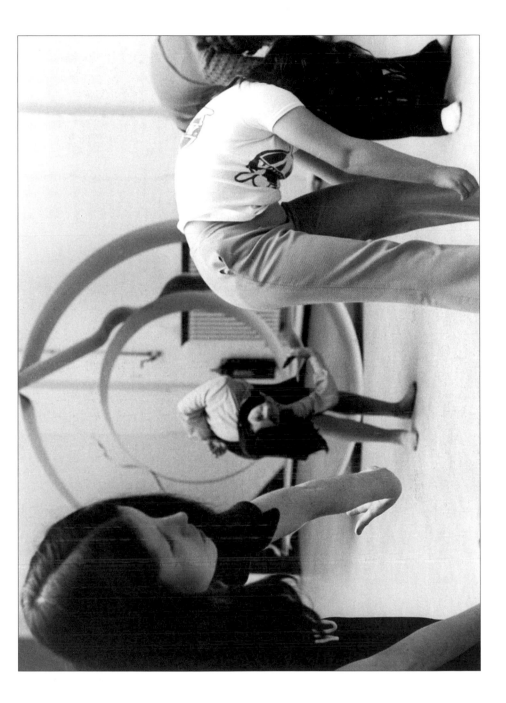

Experiments	1 Learn to differentiate between straight lines and curves, planes and angles in a sculpture – understand this through different parts of the body.

1 Learn to differentiate between straight lines and curves, planes and angles in a sculpture – understand this through different parts of the body.

2 Work in groups to create: a circle – from the circle change into as many different triangles as possible, using different levels – lying – sitting – standing – walking; orchestrate the groups so that each one represents one shape only.

3 Groups create their own sculpture: children join in one after another, everyone adding his own individual shape, touching or interlocking with the others.

4 They make symmetrical and asymmetrical sculptures – try to understand the structure of a sculpture by a mirror game – start with one part only – hands, face or legs – then involve the whole body.

5 Divide into two groups: one makes a symmetrical, the other an asymmetrical sculpture; they watch each other and make their own comments.

6 Transparent sculptures made of fibreglass create reflections and mirror shapes to which the children can react.

We finish every session by providing the children with plenty of paper and paints to express their visual impressions. As an experiment we asked one group to paint their impressions of the sculptures after simply looking at them. The other went through our movement sessions, then did their paintings. These pictures reflected an infinitely richer experience than the others.

Many classes did not finish their exploration in a single session at the Tate Gallery, but continued in their own classes writing, painting and making their own sculptures. One class sent another, and the gallery has now had many requests from school teachers to join the scheme. The programme involved children from infant, junior and maladjusted schools as well as students from Art and Drama Colleges.

7 Ways of Working

There is only one real joy in the world,
    the joy of creation.
    All other pleasures are only shadows
    wandering like strangers on earth
                    Romain Rolland

THREE WAYS TO AN UNDERSTANDING OF MOVEMENT

This chapter concerns our own perception of our body, which may be developed in terms of:

1 Purely physical awareness
2 Movement sequences
3 The creative imagination expressed in
   a. dramatic themes
   b. abstract movement

Through guided concentration, awareness of every part of the body can be sharpened separately, and in relationship to every other part. This procedure brings about a balancing of tensions and co-ordination, and encourages economy of movement.

We stress individual work and enterprise, working with each person to his or her own ability, encouraging by stimulating students to stretch themselves individually, not thinking of the body as something separate from the person to be 'kept fit'.

One of the best ways to work in movement is to work around a certain theme and develop it. We choose a subject, then try to shed light on it from different points of view, exploring as many different ways to our objective as we can find. We emphasise the importance of knowing one's own body and mind, improving the whole person and involving the whole group in an artistically meaningful way.

The following chapter is not divided into single lessons. It is an accumulation of material with which we have worked for years. It is meant to stimulate and widen the vocabulary of movement around one subject. Some parts can be used as preparation for work on voice and breathing.

The chapters on the pelvis, head, neck and eyes, sensitivity and expressiveness of the back are meant as a basis for observation of men and animals, leading to improvement of physical skills. This technique can also be applied to character studies.

Our approach is an objective one, not dependent on any particular style, aimed at creating a new dimension and quality of movement for actors and dancers.

THE PELVIS

The pelvis is the centre of the body, its strongest link, essential to a correct balance of the postural relationship. It is in a sense the driving force of the person. Here we work in an analytical way to elaborate on the theme.

Scanning whilst lying on the back

Scanning – what parts of the body are in contact with the floor? Students lie on the back on the floor. Starting with the feet: what part of the heels touches the floor? How does the pressure feel? What part of the lower leg touches the floor? At what angle to the floor do the legs lie? The back of the knees, do they touch the floor (most people cannot touch the floor without being made aware of the possibilities)? What part of the thighs touches the floor? At what angle? After having scanned both legs, compare the feeling of the right with that of the left leg. What part of the pelvis touches the floor? Move the pelvis gently without lifting it off the floor. How does the pressure vary from one side to the other, from the upper part to the lower part? Can you think of anything to improve the contact between the pelvis and the floor?

Bend both legs, put the feet on the floor, the feet beneath the knees (so that the lower leg can stand effortlessly vertically to the floor), legs parallel, open to the width of the hips. A good way to achieve this is to lift both legs off the floor with bent knees and let the feet drop on to the floor. Repeat the checking of the way the pelvis touches the floor. In this position now it is easy to feel the pelvis as a whole and in close contact with the floor. Move the pelvis up and down without lifting it off the floor; move it from side to side without lifting it off the floor; then combine both directions in one circular movement.

Now check the contact of the rest of the spine with the floor. How do the vertebrae touch the floor, how many can one feel separately? How do the shoulders touch the floor? How much pressure can be felt? How does the neck feel? Does it feel unduly tense? How do the arms feel? At what angle do they touch the floor? What parts of the hands touch the floor? Compare the feeling of each arm and shoulder? Is there a difference between right and left?

Now try to put pressure on the feet? What is the result of this simple action? The pelvis will lift itself off the floor almost automatically. Now on the way back let the spine lower itself to the floor gradually, as though trying to count the vertebrae: Repeat several times and check again the way the pelvis, spine, shoulders and arms touch the floor. Now repeat the pressure on the standing feet, but imagine that you are on a slope, therefore the direction of the pressure will not be directed vertically into the floor but at an angle of 45°. The result will be a marked lengthening of the spine before the pelvis will lift itself off the floor. This is a very simple but very effective way of elongating the spine without any conscious effort to do so.

Catposition

Now stand on all-fours, touching the floor with the hands and lower leg including the knees; open the legs as wide as the hips. In this position move the pelvis forward and backward. At first make a small movement in order to locate the feeling of the pelvis; then a larger movement to increase the flow; then move to maximum movement, gradually to feel the full range of possibility, but beware not to force the spine. Return to starting position, the back parallel to the floor. Now move the pelvis from side to side, first with a small movement, then medium, then large to maximum, again not forcing the spine.

Sitting

Sit back on the heels, move the pelvis forward and backward, again in three stages: small, medium and large movements. From this sitting position move the pelvis upward so that the body will be vertical to the floor, and sit back again on the heels, varying the speed of the movement.

Now sit in an oriental position, the legs crossed over, and move the pelvis forward and backward as far as possible.

Experimenting with movements on the floor

Let people find their own sitting positions in which it is possible to move the pelvis.

Standing

Take up a standing position, feet parallel, legs slightly bent, separated at width of hips. Move the pelvis forward and backward in three stages, small medium and large movements.

Walk in a large circle: with bent legs to free the pelvis.

Fix the pelvis at a backward position and walk forward (like an African ritual dance).

Fix the pelvis in a forward position, walking forward (like a fashion model).

Fix the pelvis forward but let it swing from side to side while walking (like a cowboy).

Experiments

Let people walk freely in the studio and create various characters by different use of the pelvis.

Walk in a circle facing the centre, stepping sideways; open, close, open, close, moving the pelvis with each step, forward and backward alternately.

Create various animals by using the pelvis only, in any position required – standing, sitting, lying and interchanging to create various animals, such as:

hen, peacock, various birds,
cat, lion, cheetah,
snake, worms, insects.

In this free adaptation other parts of the body may be included, but always start the movement from the pelvis.

Students' homework

The following are some of the titles of students' compositions following this kind of work:
Expecting a Baby
Extra hour for sleeping

When the pressure is too much for one man
Power-cut warning
The bubbles on ice still waiting for a winner in the name
    game
Father Christmas arrives at Lewis's
The bull who headed the terrible twelve
The telephone
Woman who lives in fear.

THE HEAD, NECK AND EYES

The movement of the eyes influences the function of the torso and neck muscles, and therefore organizes the movement of the whole body. We aim at improving head – neck – eye-coordination.

Lie flat on the back on the floor, keeping the eyes closed.
Scanning – how does the body lie on the floor?
What parts of the body touch the floor?
What parts press most on the floor?
What is the relationship between the head and the floor?
If the floor was soft, what shape of a mould would the head make?
Where can one feel the ears?
How far from the shoulders are the ears?
Where does one feel the tongue, how heavy does it feel?
Where do the upper and lower jaw meet? How far from the ears are they?
Where does one feel the nose?
Where does one feel the eyes?

Now imagine the neck lengthening and the head moving away from the shoulders. This does not involve action, but letting the imagination influence the body.

Now check where the tongue is; it should be resting on the lower jaw touching the lower front teeth.

Now move the eyes, while still closed, from side to side, then up and down.

Now move the head to the right, keeping the eyes to the left; do the same to the other side.

Now check the relationship between the different parts of the body. The head and neck to shoulders, the shoulders to the pelvis, the pelvis to the legs. Now imagine the distance lengthening from heels to pelvis, from pelvis to shoulders, and again from shoulders to head and neck.

Sit in an oriental position, legs crossed in front. Rotate the head to the right and back to the centre; repeat ten to fifteen times. Be aware that with each rotation, if correctly applied, the head will move a little further without any special effort. Now compare the feeling of this side to the side that has not moved.

Repeat with the other side to balance the feeling.

Now move the head sideways, moving the ear towards the shoulder, keeping the eyes forward. Pay attention to the halfcircle the tip of nose draws in space.

Move the head down, back and up, being careful not to contract the neck.

Rotate the head to the right, move it down and up in that position; same to the other side.

Now imagine the tip of the nose to be a compass and draw imaginary circles on an imaginary sheet of paper; make distinctions between small and large circles.

Experiments	Make phrases using any combination of movements suggested so far. Phrases should be of at least four or five combinations in varying rhythms, and repeatable. The combinations can be made in any sitting position desired.
	Sit in couples in any desired position, make conversation using the head, neck and eyes.
A character or a mood	Vary the type of conversation, making the movements express a character or a mood: shy, extroverted, nervous, aggressive, determined characters; happy, melancholy, sulking, joking, sad moods.
Experiments preferably after a visit to a zoo	In standing position use various combinations of the movements of the pelvis, the head and neck.
	Split up into individuals, creating animals using the head, neck and pelvic movements.

Once established move the animals in space.

Specialise and restrict the type of animal into:

    birds only;

    animals walking on all-fours;

    reptiles.

Students' Project
How King Charles I lost his head
LOST
One head, complete with crown and beard. If thou findst it, please return to King Charles King
Apply   Buckingham Palace Londonne after curfew
Rewarde

FOUND
One Royal head minus crown, answers to the name of Rover
Apply   Oliver Cromwell
                                         Houses of Parliament
Tired of the same old eccentrics?
Afraid of losing *your* head?
Why worry, when there's 'Hire-a-Head!'
Realistic heads made to suit any pocket or collar.
Don't be caught out.
Make sure you get your Hire-a-Head *today*!
Satisfaction guaranteed or your money back.
Strike while the blood is hot!

We set as homework, to create a character from the 17th century in mime. After this was presented we asked for an attractive poster to invite audiences to the performance.
     The above is one sample.

IMPOSING BODILY RESTRICTIONS

Patterns of work

From an
oriental position

The idea is to explore unusual movements, using the floor as our base without standing on it.

a. Begin by sitting on the floor in an oriental position, legs crossed.
     Now move the legs in any way possible without touching the floor.
     Observe the difference between moving the legs from the hipjoint only, without bending the knees, and doing the same bending the knees: a much greater variety of movement is possible if the knees are bent.

     Next start again in the same position. Ask the students to draw shapes with their legs in the air. They discover that their whole approach to and feeling for the movements will differ: the feet start playing a much more active and vital part, the movements become smaller in size, more differentiated in their expression.

Music can be used to emphasise the rhythmical nature of these movements.

From lying flat on the back	b. Start lying on the back, having to move the body without allowing the legs to touch the floor. Students find themselves turning, rolling – they travel across the floor in any direction, changing from back to front to side in many ways. The task is made even harder if students are not allowed to touch the floor with the arms – this is a great restriction and we need to rely mainly on movements of the pelvis.
From standing – going down and up	c. Now try to discover various ways of getting down to the floor from a standing position. Start in 'neutral position'. Bend in the hip joints, knees, ankles, add the toe joints at the ball of the foot until the knees touch the floor – shift the weight backwards and get up again.
Changed ways of using the body to go down to the floor and up	The first task is to go down to the floor as before; then shift the pelvis to the floor, keeping the back straight, extending the legs over the side and touching the floor with a straight back. Here the hip joints will have to be used extensively, the back kept elongated, head and neck extended and free to rotate sideways, the breath free – movement will be flowing, free and convincing, whatever the restrictions imposed.
Theme and variations	d. Now try different ways: first use one leg behind the other, changing the base from a symmetrical to an asymmetrical one, but still maintaining the straight back.

The last variation is to lower ourselves to the floor without imposing any restrictions on the use of the back, allowing the torso to bend and curve freely, but varying the speed and rhythm of the movement.

This exercise too can be accompanied by music, or

students can accompany themselves by speaking words, poems, speeches from plays.

Students'
homework
produced the
following titles

Cat's Cradle
Origami
Seaweed
Tick-Tack Clockwork
Ice Symmetry
Rolling in Money

MOBILITY OF THE HIP JOINT

What can be done with the hip joint?

In this section we discover that we can greatly increase mobility in the hip joint by directing our awareness at separating the legs from the back – releasing superfluous tension – increasing the expressive power of the body. We also discover a new aspect of our relationship to space, and this can be used for further character studies.

Patterns of work

This involves working with the back (pelvis and torso as one unit) on different bases.

Small base: feet parallel touching each other

First stand on a small base with straight legs. Bend the back straight from the hip joint without curves and return to upright position. Repeat this into the eight directions of the vertical planes from (0) to (7) (see chapter on Space), forward – backward – sideways.
At first the bending is done without changing the direction of the eyes, which always face the front (0) plane.

Repeat all the movements with a rotation in the hip joint – now the eyes will travel around with the movement.

Repeat the same movements with bent legs to gain a wider range of movement.

Medium base: feet parallel at width of hips

Next proceed to a medium base, repeating all the previous movements. Start with straight legs without rotating the hip joint. Gradually lift restrictions: allow rotation in the hip joint; bend the legs – an almost infinite number of movement combinations is possible.

Large base: legs apart as far as possible with parallel feet	Repeat all previous movement combinations on a large base. We discover that mobility increases. The larger the base – the greater the freedom to move.
Variations with open hip joint	In contrast to the previous parallel position use the 'turn out' – the opening (rotation outward) of the hip joint. It is necessary to stress the importance of the correct relationship when bending the knees: bend the leg so that you can draw a vertical line from the knee to the space between the big toe and second toe – where Indian sandals have a strap holding the foot. All previous movements are possible in this way.
Variations with closed hip joint	All movements can be repeated with closed hip joint – with thighs turned in at the hip joint.
Variations with free combinations	It is possible to work with any free combination, discovering mainly the difference between symmetrical, parallel and asymmetrical shapes.
Variations with curved back	Now we have arrived at a point where we can 'let go' of the back, meaning we can round it, curve it – concave or

142

convex – forward, sideways, backward in any way we like.

Arms added

Now we can add the arms, continuing the line of the back, moving with the direction of the pelvis, moving against the pelvis and torso.

The accent is on continuing the shape and direction of the body.

Variations in sitting positions

All the preceeding exploration of the relationship between back and space by using the hip joint can be done in sitting positions.

First the oriental position – symmetrical, with legs crossed in front of the body.

Then in the Greek position – asymmetrical, with both legs bent to one side, the foot of one leg touching the front of the knee of the other leg.

Finally in the Egyptian position – symmetrical, sitting on the heels, knees and feet touching the floor, weight on the ball of the foot.

Dramatic interpretations

a. We developed these experiments into team work on Egyptian wall reliefs. To inspire students we used reproductions and slides.
b. On other occasions grotesque social comments grew out of the work.
c. And it has been the basis for character studies.

EXTENDING THE BACK MUSCLES

This section accents the technical aspect of our work: elongating the back by lengthening the extensor muscles and co-ordinating arm and leg movements.

It is important to be aware of the proper use of the body.

a. Start, standing with legs parallel, width of the hips. Ask people to touch the floor with the palms of the hands – this is difficult for some.

Allow people to bend legs, so that everyone can touch the floor.

In this position straighten legs alternately; think of the extension of the leg as upward rather than back-

144

ward. (Head and neck are untensed, tongue hangs freely in the mouth.)

Sit back on the heels and rest.

b. Raise pelvis as high as possible upwards not backwards, leave head hanging freely, untensed neck.

Stay down, shift weight forward and backward, without moving the feet or hands from their contact point on the floor.

Sit back on the heels to rest.

c. From previous position (hands and feet touching the floor) walk on the hands as far away from the feet as possible without raising the heels. Shift weight forward and backward.

Touch floor with feet and palms – walk backwards from the hands – touch the floor with the heels after each step.

Sit back and rest.

d. Start again from the position with feet and hands touching the floor; walk on hands away from the feet, eventually lifting the heels off the floor until stretching out on the abdomen – the whole front of the body touching the floor.

Start walking backwards from the lying position by bending the toes so that the weight of the body is transferred first to the balls of the feet through lifting the pelvis upwards, supporting the front of the body on the palms of the hands, and watching that the lower arm is placed precisely vertically to the floor to enable the bone to carry most of the weight. Walk until the whole weight can be placed on the feet, releasing the hands off the floor, then straightening the body up to standing position.

Repeat in reverse: start from standing position, drop the head and neck forwards, then follow the weight of the head towards the floor until the hands touch the floor again. Repeat as often as necessary. Repeat – but on moving backwards don't straighten up, shift weight backward, first on the heels, then lower the pelvis towards the floor. Straighten the

145

spine on the floor (leaving hands off the floor of course) until lying on the back.

e. Try again to touch the floor with the palms of the hands, keeping the knees straight: first by bending the body forwards from the hip joint; second by stretching the arms vertically upwards with the palms flexed, thinking of separating the back away from the legs – elongating the spine, balancing the head on top of the spine, then lowering the back away from the hip joint, keeping it straight as long as possible, return to starting position by straightening the spine one vertebra after the other.

f. Sit on the floor – space between legs the width of the hips, placing the feet in front of the body with feet flexed to maximum, keeping them parallel, and putting the hands over the feet so as to hold the feet at the ball.

From this position start walking on the heels forward, keeping the torso attached to the upper legs as long as possible.

Repeat several times walking forward and backward until the legs can straighten.

Gradually move the hands forward over the feet according to individual ability – keep knees straight. Straighten legs simultaneously, then alternately one leg bent and one straight.

Sit up straight – legs straight on the floor – body and legs create a 90° angle. Push the arms upwards towards the ceiling – extending the line of the back, hands flexed, palms upwards.

From this position bend the back to become parallel to the legs, as far as possible touching the toes or ball of the foot – repeat several times.

Touch the feet as previously, keep knees straight, flex and stretch the feet in that position.

g. Bring the legs upwards and over the head until they touch the floor behind the head.

After touching the floor with the feet, open legs, and stand on the floor with the ball of the foot – bend and stretch the knees:

147

both knees at once;
alternate knees.

Repeat the same with legs closed – bend and stretch, thinking that the heel moves away from the pelvis.

Combine the last two movements: straight legs behind the head touching the floor – bring legs in front of the body, push the arms upwards, hands flexed – bend forward over the legs – touch the toes or ball of the foot with the hands.

Check after every few movement combinations the original starting position.

BALANCE AND CO-ORDINATION

By creating unusual off-balance situations one can use instability to lead to co-ordination. Let students orientate themselves to find their own balance, out of which emerge imaginative interpretations.

Ask students to run in the studio, at a given sign stop, and touch the floor with the palm of one hand.

Repeat with the back of the hand; repeat, touching the floor with one hand and one lower leg (not counting the supporting leg); repeat with change of sides; repeat with free choice of hand and lower leg.

Let people walk or run, at a given sign touch the floor with varying numbers of limbs, numbered according to teacher's discretion, as 3, 6, 7, 5 etc.; in a static position touch the floor with a given number of limbs, preferably an uneven number, such as two hands and one arm; in this chosen position move as many different parts of the body as possible: pelvis, head and shoulders, torso.

Every student has to make a sequence, touching the floor with various parts of the body in a succession of numbers, say from 1–7, reversing the process, then creating a phrase going forward and backward; repeat the last sequence at varying speeds, crescendo-decrescendo.

Touch the floor with as many parts of the body as possible; gradually reduce the parts that touch the floor, eventually arriving sitting on the pelvic bone or standing on one leg, thus having to balance the body.

Off-balance work

Use the starting position, standing on one leg only, to imitate birdlike movements, or butterflies or material qualities such as cloth, paper, wood, as listed in the chapter on 'Imagination'.

Standing on one leg, move the gesture leg in different ways: legato, staccato, near the body, away from the body, paying attention to the directions as in chapter on 'Space'.

Sit on the pelvic bone. Move legs and/or arms in different ways: legato, staccato, one leg or arm legato, the other staccato, near the centre of the body, away from the body, arm and leg in one direction, arm and leg in different directions (refer to chapter on 'Space').

The last two exercises can be varied by suggesting that students draw shapes in space.

Further development: movement with advanced students can include the limiting of the movement into use of the gesture leg with hip joint open, or hip joint closed; or accenting the importance of the use of the ankle joint.

The same experiments can be made by sitting on a chair.

149

Work in couples

Balance the
body in off-
balance
positions
(lability)

Students run in the studio, and
touch each other with one limb only:
    hand to hand,
    lower arm to lower arm,
    knee to knee,
    thigh to thigh,
    lower leg to lower leg;
    one person's hand touches the other person's foot,
    lower leg,
    knee or thigh;
    sole to sole of the foot.

People chose a number of combinations, standing on one or two legs, and remain touching each other in a static position, then move the rest of the body to complement each other's movements.

Homework: prepare a composition inspired by these experiments, giving it an abstract or dramatic title.

SENSITIVITY AND EXPRESSIVENESS OF THE BACK

This section explores and develops imaginatively the sense of touch and shape. We illuminate the back from

new aspects, so that emotional experience can be expressed in the back alone.

Every actor and dancer should go through this experience.

Patterns of work Students start sitting in couples, the backs touching, the eyes closed. First they try to become 'acquainted' with their partners' back by coming into contact with the back only – no other part of the body is used at this point. No commands are given by the tutor, the participants concerned are left to themselves. No speech is used, but students are free to move in any way they wish: forward, backward, sideways; to bend their backs, stretch, lie on the floor, get up – all as long as they keep contact with their partners with at least part of the back.

Then they try to produce sounds, and let them travel down their backs: it is fascinating to feel each other's vibrations and is sometimes also a great help in voice-production. The voice experiment may equally be done with the backs of the heads touching each other – all the resonances of sound should be noticeable. This exercise greatly improves breathing.

Next students can take different roles: one partner

may sit in an oriental or any other position, while the other partner touches his back with the idea of making him react to stimulus, and thus increase the flexibility and sensitivity of the back as an independent part of the body.

A larger number of people can now be involved. One person stands on all fours (weight of the body on hands and lower leg) while a number of people touch his back, and he has to guess how many. This is harder than one would think. Then, if the people in the group are well acquainted with each other, let the person standing on all fours, preferably with closed eyes, guess who is touching him.

After having 'warmed up' in this way the group should be ready for expressive work. Let the back express different emotions – this can be done by students standing with their backs to the tutor or audience, sitting on chairs, sitting on the floor, or using any prop or scenery available.

We have had students act the following: laughing, funny, itching, nervous, giggling, curious, crying, desperate, dying, sad, hopeless, angry, wounded,

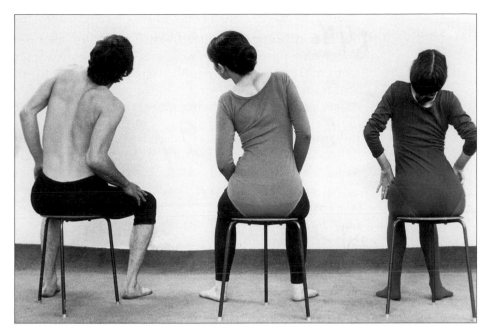

153

paralysed, sinister, afraid, insecure, shy, stupid.

From this improvised individual work one can develop whole-group improvisations, working on scenes from a Greek play, a ritual, a crowd reacting to an orator, a group following a disappearing person or object, people carrying heavy objects etc.

Projects Individual homework may be given to work from the improvised experience into a movement composition with a life of its own.

Our students have also developed projects around plays, such as:

Look Back in Anger by John Osborne

Yerma by F. G. Lorca

Six Characters in Search of an Author by Pirandello

8 Space

THE CIRCLE

While the square is closely connected with man – with construction, with architecture and building forms, lettering etc., the circle is related to the divine. Since ancient times the circle has represented eternity, for it has neither beginning nor end. An old text says that god is a circle whose centre is everywhere, but whose circumference is nowhere. The circle is essentially a dynamic figure: it is the basis of all rotary movements and of all vain searches for perpetual motion.

One person stands in the centre, and imagines a horizontal circle around him. This horizontal circle is divided into an infinite number of vertical planes, but for convenience's sake the work in the beginning stages will be broken down into arcs of 45°, eight of which combine to make the 360° of the circle.

Patterns of work From the centre of the circle the limbs – arms and legs – work in different-sized sections of the circle.

The person standing will move the arms in arcs of 45° up to 180°, which is the highest point that can be reached by using the arms only. The legs will then make movements in arcs of up to 90°, which for our purpose is enough (well-trained dancers can sometimes reach 180°.) Then he will make the same movements lying on the floor. First use the arms only, gliding along the floor; then use the legs gliding along the floor; then start lifting the arms in different directions; then lift the legs in different directions; then glide the arms and legs together, the limbs on one side of the body first, one arm and leg moving towards and away from each other; then use the opposite arm and leg, moving first in the same direction, then in opposite directions.

155

This exercise is a good opportunity for paying attention to simultaneous and co-ordinated uses of various parts of the body – be careful not to let the movements interfere with the breathing.

Next start lifting the arms off the floor in the same progression, moving always in arcs of 45°; then do the same with the legs, keeping the whole lumbar region (small of the back) on the floor.

Return to the standing position. Up to now all movements have taken place in the shoulder and hip joints only – the elbow, wrist, knee or ankle joints have not been used.

Now we shall use the whole range of joints and let the arms swing. Having first analysed the parts we shall use the circle as a whole and move rhythmically with differing accents: making a circle and a half, two circles and a half, three circles and a quarter etc. An infinity of variations is possible.

Now we shall start combining the two elements, the standing and the lying, by dividing the group into couples and letting them move in their own combinations.

Next we add another dimension by seating one person on the floor, working with all the elements so far discovered. For this the pelvis and the torso too have to be brought into action.

Students can now prepare their own compositions at home.

Elements experienced

Clarification of the concept quantities of movement in space. The combination and co-ordination of arm and leg movements. Co-operation in space between two and more people. The circle in sections and as a whole. The circle in different positions in space. The circle in relation to gravity.

With this work an exceptional amount of work is done on the joints, greatly increasing their flexibility. Indeed working on shapes and rhythms in this way we do not need mechanical exercises.

Students' homework | The following is the choreographic idea of one of our students, evolved following work on the concepts of circle and space.

Spinning, weaving and disintegration | One of our students came up with the idea of spinning and weaving as the basis for a project, the cloth then wearing thin and finally tearing to shreds.

We started by improvising on each of the elements separately – everyone making an individual composition at home. These were pooled; we edited them; and finally organised the whole group into a choreography. Everyone entered the stage with spinning movements, continued in couples, opened out into a square of weaving movements, then, using fixation of plane movements, united as one piece of cloth. They finally disintegrated again into individual shreds and were swept away by one person with a big broom.

Division of Space

The aim in evolving a system for the division of space is to clarify concepts of space, rather than wander aimlessly in it. This does not limit space to any exterior shape, such as a square stage; for our starting point is a centre that can expand into any form.

This system of division of space can be applied in various ways. We use mainly two forms:

a. The person's front is the zero, wherever he faces and moves with him.
b. We decide on a zero position in space and relate the moving people to it. Zero can be anywhere – a studio wall; the opening of a proscenium-arch stage; or a street corner.

The movements will be related to space rather than to people.

A person stands in the centre of an imaginary circle. For our purpose we divide the circle into eight sections of 45° each, we number them as follows (based on the Noa Eshkol and Abraham Wachmann system of movement notation): if the front is 0, then numbering clockwise the sections are 1, 2, 3, 4, 5, 6, 7.

157

With reference to the person's body:

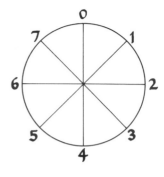

0 is front
4 is back
2 is right
6 is left
1 is diagonally (forward) between 0 and 2
3 is diagonally (backwards) between 2 and 4
5 is diagonally (backwards) between 4 and 6
7 is diagonally (forward) between 6 and 0.

The significance of this approach is that the division of space is connected with the centre of the person, therefore not dependent on the shape of the room (stage, studio, outdoors).

Application

Students are asked to walk into any of the above directions, preferably starting in order of number; four steps into the direction and four steps back to centre.

On the same principle: walk between 0 and 4 – four steps forward facing 0, four steps backwards to the neutral centre position, then four steps into 4 facing 4 (the body turns 180°), and back to centre neutral position.

Now walk into 0 and back to centre,
        into 2 and back to centre,
        into 4 and back to centre,
        into 6 and back to centre,
        and again into 0, repeating several times.

Then reverse the process:
        into 0 and back to centre,
        into 6 and back to centre
        into 4 and back to centre
        into 2 and back to centre,
        into 0 and repeat several times.

Now use the whole scale walking three, four or five steps in each direction and back centre, being precise about facing the direction we move into and the size of the steps, so that each beginning starts on the same spot.

Having explored the whole scale, limit the movements to the diagonals, unevenly numbered (the directions being spaced at 45° angles, there are 90° angles between diagonals): Starting from zero position, facing 0, move

> into 1 and back to centre,
> into 3 and back to centre,
> into 5 and back to centre,
> into 7 and back to centre.

Work in couples
Two people start facing 0 and 1 respectively, each working at angles of 90°: one walks into directions 0, 2, 4, 6, the other into directions 1, 3, 5, 7.

Alternatively, one person can walk into each of the eight directions, while the other walks into the unevenly numbered directions at the same time: the result is that while one person turns a single circle, the other can get around twice.

This exercise can be done in any number of variations.

Head movements
The head can move clearly in the following ways: forward and backward in one plane, (0) to (4) to (0); sideways between planes (2) and (6), and in the horizontal plane, in rotation. These movements may be interpreted as saying: 'yes', 'no, no', 'maybe', and can be combined in any desired way.

This method of work will increase and define orientation in space in a way especially useful for actors: for the way a person uses his head is greatly indicative of character.

Shift of weight in space
Ask a student to stand in the centre in zero position, then shift the weight into 0 until he is on the verge of falling. He saves himself by thrusting out one leg, which carries the weight of the body – the body should make one diagonal line in space, like a lunge. Return to zero position.

Then shift the weight into 2, weight on right leg;

159

return to zero, weight on both legs evenly distributed.

In the same way shift the weight into 6, falling on to left leg; return to zero, weight evenly distributed on both legs.

Make sure that in each direction the body draws one diagonal line.

When these directions are mastered, shift the weight backwards, falling into 4, still making one diagonal line with the body.

Until now the front of the body has not changed, eyes always to the front (facing 0).

The same movements into 2 and 6 can now be repeated, changing the front of the body by turning the torso into the direction of fall.

The movement is then repeated into directions 1, 2, 3, 4; before each new movement come back to centre, shifting the weight from the right leg back to both. To the left with the left leg, the movement will start with 7, then go to 6, 5, 4, etc., the weight of the body shifted each time on to the leg, then back to centre on to both.

Before each movement take care to achieve maximum elongation in the spine so that the body works at its lightest with a freely released neck and no superfluous tension.

Work in couples

Two partners start facing 0. One partner goes around the scale starting in 1, the other starting in 7 so that a symmetrical pattern is achieved.

Two partners start by facing 0, then move in the same directions, but one moves with a change of front, the other without. This makes people aware of different sensations and different awareness of space even while they are using a similar kind of movement.

Exploration of Space

Rhythmic and Dramatic Variations:

a. Tell students to spread out in space, walking, running or jumping. Give different rhythmic accents:

$$\acute{1}\,2\,3\,4, 1\,\acute{2}\,3\,4, 1\,2\,\acute{3}\,4, 1\,2\,3\,\acute{4}\,\,\text{\textsf{L}},$$

Then ask them to make short phrases, using any combination of the three differing ways of moving in space (walking, running, jumping).

When a phrase has been decided upon, take it through a number of variations, such as changing height, time and direction.

Incorporating dramatic ideas

b. Incorporate ideas into phrases created before: start with advance – retreat. These in turn can be used in variations:

> friendly – unfriendly
> aggressively – fearfully
> hesitantly – gradually
> exuberantly – despairingly
> victoriously – defeatedly.

Fix two points in space: Move from one to the other in the shortest possible way.

Moving between given points in space

c. Move from one to the other in various, longer ways: these can be totally undefined, or they can be limited to curved lines, sharp angles, obtuse angles.

Variations

d. Move by advancing and retreating in a given ratio:

> 3 steps forward 1 step back
> 4 steps forward 2 steps back
> 5 steps forward 3 steps back

alternating with

> 4 steps forward 5 steps backward
> 3 steps forward 4 steps backward

Using two-dimensional designs

e. Create a space pattern by drawing a design on paper, or, if available, on a blackboard. Then use the pattern for movement in space, forbidding the feet to touch the floor; thus forcing movements into crawls, rolls, somersaults.

Awareness of other people's moves

f. Let people move freely in any direction of their choice, but allowing them to change from one plane to the other only in the centre of the circle where all planes meet. The condition is that not more than one person can change in the centre at a time, and that nobody is allowed to stand still. Therefore people

161

have to be aware of each other and to have the ability to sense their partners' pacing, particularly if a musical background accompanies the interplay.

Fixation of the movement of one limb in one plane

g. A student is told to walk in one direction – on one plane – and at the same time move one arm in a whole circle in another plane. This creates interesting spatial relationships, and makes for co-ordination and unusual work in the joints.

We discover possibilities of using parts of the body to create shapes, enabling these parts to 'lead separate lives', which can be used by an intelligent choreographer to accent dramatic situations.

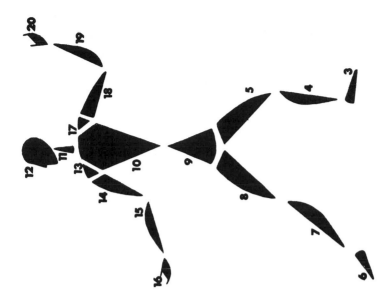

		20
	Hand	20
	Forearm	19
Left	Upper Arm	18
	Shoulder	17
	Hand	16
	Forearm	15
Right	Upper Arm	14
	Shoulder	13
	Head	12
	Neck	11
	Torso (upper part)	10
	Pelvis	9
	Thigh	8
Right	Lower Leg	7
	Foot	6
	Thigh	5
Left	Lower Leg	4
	Foot	3
	Weight	2
	Front	1

Time →

Score

163

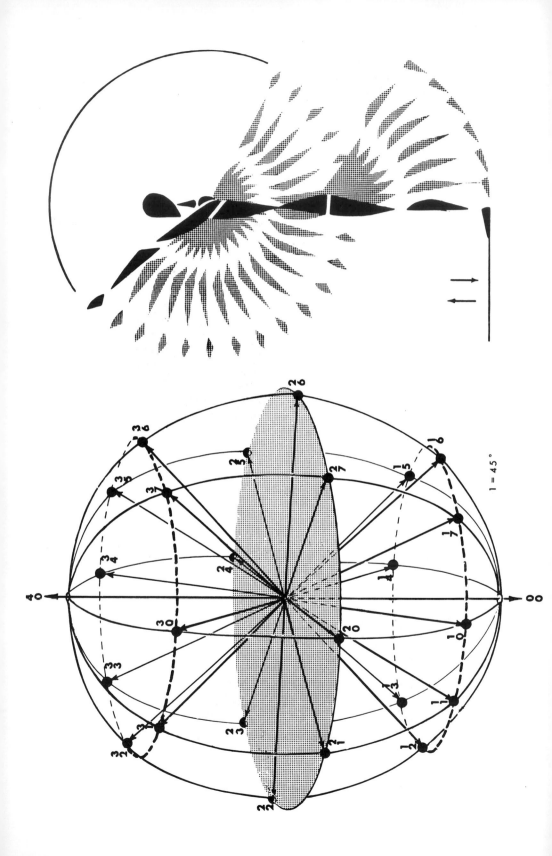

1 = 45°

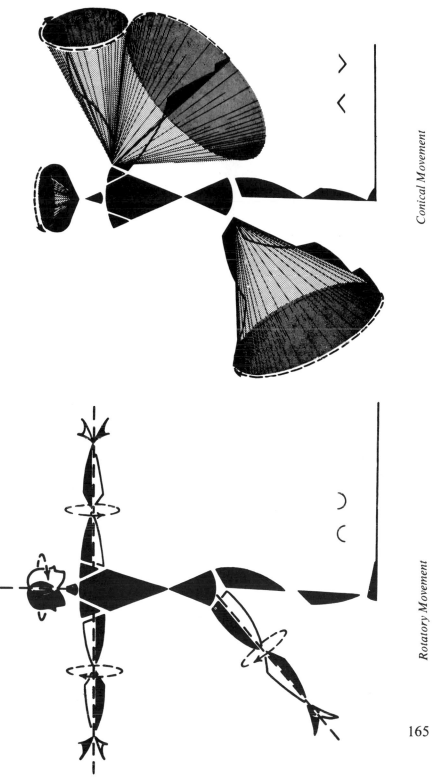

Conical Movement

Rotatory Movement

Analysis of a Position of the Body

Contact of Parts of the body with the ground

166

Appendix – a Sample Curriculum

Movement Context
The following is part of the curriculum of a three-year drama course at degree level:

General

We wish to produce a balanced person who has a working discipline, can use his/her body and voice freely. Is co-operative, open minded, flexible, has a curiosity about life and is willing to work hard at any task set. Who can take responsibility for his actions, is able to love and receive love, in short fully human. Is able to use his imagination and creative powers.

First Year
Aim: Awareness of self through awareness of shape, sensory perception and rhythm in individual studies and group projects.

1st term

Basic Awareness of the body
Structural concepts:
    The skeleton
    The vertebral column
    Joints
    Posture: sitting – standing – walking

Movement Awareness – Practical Application
Work on the back – bending – lifting – carrying – breathing.

Basic Sensory Perception
Touch – Sound – Sight.

Imagination and Creativity
Colour, Shape and Movement: Students' own drawings stimulating movement shapes and rhythms. Painting with colours – movement inspired by colours – dynamic concepts.
    Use of materials to change the shape and character of the body and its movements.

167

Assessment: on the culmination of the term's work, in a showing of prepared projects – individual, group work. Students are judged at showing and by continuous assessment throughout the term.

2nd term

Integrated Concepts

Eutony – organisation and proper use of the body – dynamic relaxation – reversability – observing while absorbing – lightness and floating.

Ways of Working

Working around a theme as opposed to the idea of working on set exercises.

Using sound – speech – movement – percussion instruments.

Space

Principles of space structure – movement in the joints – amount of movement – concepts of symmetry, asymmetry, parallel. Quantity of movement – man in the centre of a circle and in the centre of a sphere – dividing 360° into eight units of 45° each.

Shifting the weight of the body in space – incorporating ideas into and giving emotional content to directions.

Sensory Perception

Further Exploration.

In general continuation of first term's work with added stimulus of mime, masks, props and possibly costume. Use of poetry and certain aspects of early dramatic forms to be recreated in movement.

Assessment: continuous on work progress throughout the term, then on showing at the end of term.

3rd term

The whole first year is aimed towards increasing self-awareness. We learn to trust and know ourselves and the people we work with; we also learn to react to varying situations gaining a deeper insight into our own world and character.

The third term adds to students' knowledge of the

function of the body and basic principles of movement, and the exact form of this work depends largely on the inherent group dynamic of each individual year. As we do not teach any mechanical skills the particular contents and expression largely depends on the members of the group.

Basic movement notation is taught during the last term.

Assessment: a written paper (2 hours) on principles of movement and movement notation.

The final year's grade is based on a summary of three terms' assessments.

Second Year

1st term
Exploration of character in mime in solo and group situations, based for example on the Commedia dell'Arte characters (these will have been studied in Forms of Drama).

Beginning of period movement – developing a sense of style.

Basic terms of classical ballet explained.

Assessment: each student will prepare 2 five-minute character studies (compositions) and a longer group project incorporating one of the characters. These studies should incorporate a defined space composition, strengthening the first year's basic concepts. Emphasis also to be placed on dynamic-rhythmic development of the characters.

2nd term
Period movement taught through historical dances – with live accompaniment – costume desired.

Continuation of the principles of the classical ballet.

Deepening of the sensory perception and the imaginative approaches started off in the first year.

At some time during the second year a combined movement and voice project will take place.

Assessment on prepared dances.

3rd term
The movement will be exposed to the discipline of a full-scale performance in intimate surroundings. This will give the experience of compositional laws and stress the necessity for precision and defined shapes.

169

Assessment will be on the contribution to the show, included in the continuous assessment throughout the year.

The latter part of term will be less intense, to allow for the pressure of the customary public performances.

Third Year

Study of the T'ai Chi Ch'uan – the ancient Chinese system of movement. It has as its goal the achievement of health and tranquility by means of a 'way of movement', characterised by a technique of moving slowly and continuously without strain, through a varied sequence of contrasting forms that create stable vitality with calmness, balanced strength with flexibility, controlled energy with awareness. It is a synthesis of form and function. It is an art-in-action for the doer. Because every movement is anticipated by the mind, patience and control of temper develop without effort. . . . 'it is when tranquility is perfect that the human faculties display all their resources, because they are enlightened by reason and sustained knowledge.' The structures are so varied as to bring into play every part of the body from the smallest joint to the largest muscle.

One public performance of a movement orientated show is to be given in the third year with the use of multimedia – aiming at 'total theatre'.

Unarmed combat is practised regularly by all students throughout the whole three-year course, and fencing instruction is given.

Consolidation and practical application of movement principles in the performance situation is one of the main objects of the third year.

Assessment: on movement in public productions of plays and general attitude. A musical or a play including dancing is to be included.

In addition students should present an individual or small-group composition for assessment. This will give the opportunity to students who are more movement – than acting – orientated, to present their work. It is also possible to present a thesis that is either movement or dance orientated.

Two-Hour Examination Paper

1 Basic Awareness of the Body:
    Answer two of either a, b, c, or d only:
    a. describe the structure of the skeleton
    b. describe the curvatures of the spine
    c. what is the function of the joints?
    d. posture: how should we stand?
        how should we sit?
        how should we walk?

2 Principles of Working:
    Answer the following:
    a. what is Eutony?
    b. what is Co-ordination?
    c. what is Reversibility?
    d. what is Elongation?

3 Movement Awareness:
    Answer two of the following:
    a. How do we measure amount of movement?
    b. How do we work to improve the function of the back?
    c. What is the correct way of using the back while lifting, bending and carrying weight?
    d. Suggest three different ways of work on breathing.

4 Sensory Perception:
    Answer one of the following:
    a. Why do we work with closed eyes?
    b. Describe a personal experience.
    c. Give a few examples of work on touch and trust.

5 Space:
    Answer one of the following:
    a. What is the principle of dividing space?
    b. Describe the dramatic use of space.

6 Imagination:
    Give two or three examples of imaginative work.

Bibliography

Movement and Dance

Cunningham, Merce, *Changes: Notes on Choreography*, Something Else Press, New York, 1968

Delza, Sophie, *T'ai Chi Ch'uan*, Cornerstone Library, New York, 1961

Eshkol, Noa and Wachmann, Abraham, *Movement Notation*, Weidenfeld and Nicolson London, 1958

H'Doubler, Margaret N., *Dance: a Creative Art Experience*, University of Wisconsin, Press, 1968

Her Majesty's Stationary Office, *Moving and Growing*, London, 1972

Horst, L. and Russel C., *Modern Dance Forms*, Dance Horizons, New York, 1961

Houghton W. F. (editor), *Educational Gymnastics*, London County Council, 1964

Kleist, Heinrich von, *Aufsatz ueber das Marionettentheater*, Studien und Interpretationen. Berlin:E. Schmidt Ver 1967

Kirstein, Lincoln and Stuart, Muriel, *The Classic Ballet*, Alfred Knopf, New York, 1952

Laban, Rudolf, *The Mastery of Movement*, Macdonald and Evans, London, 1971

Leatherman, LeRoy, *Martha Graham*, Faber and Faber, London 1961

Murray, Ruth L., *Dance in Elementary Education*, Harper and Broth, New York, 1953

North, Marion, *Movement Education*, Temple Smith, London 1973

Noverre, Jean G., *Letters on Dancing and Ballets*, republished by Dance Horizon, New York, 1966

Percival, John, *Experimental Dance*, Studio Vista, London, 1971

Preston, Valerie, *A Handbook for Modern Educational Dance*, Macdonald and Evans, London, 1963

Sachs, Kurt, *World History of the Dance*, Seven Arts Publishers, New York, 1952

Shawn, Ted, *Every little Movement*, published by the author, 1954

Sorell, Walter, *The Dance through the Ages*, Thames and Hudson, London, 1967

Drama

Artaud, Antonin, *The Theatre and its Double*, Calder and Boyars, London, 1970

Benedetti, Robert L., *The Actor at Work*, Prentice Hall N. J. 1970

Brook, Peter, *The Empty Space*, Macgibbon and Kee, London, 1968

Chekhov, Michael, *To the Actor on the Technique of Acting*, Harper and Row, London, 1953

Grotowski, Jerzy, *Towards a Poor Theatre*, Odin Teatrets Forlag, Denmark, 1968

Hartnoll, Phyllis, *A Concise History of the Theatre*, Thames and Hudson, London, 1968

Morrison, Hugh, *Directing in the Theatre*, Pitman Publishing, London, 1973

Lessac, Arthur, *The Use and Training of the Human Voice*, D.B.S. Publications, New York, 1967

Kostelanetz, R., *The Theatre of Mixed Means*, Pitman Publishing, London, 1970

Roose-Evans, James, *Experimental Theatre*, Studio Vista, London, 1970

Slade, Peter, *Child Drama*, University of London Press, 1954

Spolin, Viola, *Improvisation for the Theatre*, North Western University Press Illinois, 1963

Stanislavski, Constantin, *Building a Character*, U.P. Paperback, London, 1968

Tomkins, Calvin, *Five Masters of the Avant-Garde*, The Viking Press, New York, 1962

Walker, Kathrine S., *Eyes on Mime*, The John Day Co., New York, 1969

Way, Brian, *Development through Drama*, Longman, London, 1967

Toita, Yasuji, *Kabuki, The Popular Theatre*, Weatherhill/Tankosha, New York, 1970

Anatomy

F. M. Alexander, *The Use of the Self*, Methuen, London 1932

Barlow, Wilfred, *The Alexander Principle*, Victor Gollancz, London, 1973

Darwin, Charles, *The Expression of the Emotions in Man and Animals*, J. Murray, London, 1872

Feldenkrais, Dr. Moshe, *Body and Mature Behaviour*, Routledge and Kegan Paul, London, 1949

Feldenkrais, Dr. Moshe, *Awareness through Movement*, Harper and Row, London, New York, 1972

Edited by Hamilton, W. J., *Textbook of Human Anatomy*, MacMillan, 1956

Rowett, H. G. Q., *Basic Anatomy and Physiology*, John Murray, London, 1959

Todd, Mabel Elsworth, *The Thinking Body*, Dance Horizons, New York, 1937

Psychology

Fagan, Joen and Shepherd, Lee (editors), *Gestalt Therapy Now*, Harper & Row, New York, London, 1970

Fromm, Erich, *Fear of Freedom*, Routledge & Kegan Paul, London, 1942

Jung, C. G., *Man and his Symbols*, Aldus Books Ltd., London, 1964

Koestler, Arthur, *The Act of Creation*, Pan Books Ltd., London, 1964

Laing, R. D., *The Divided Self*, Penguin Books, Pelican Edition, 1965

Maslow, A. H., *Motivation and Personality*, Harper and Row, New York, 1970

Neumann, Erich, *Art and the Creative Unconscious*, Princeton Univ. Press, N.J. 1971

Piaget, J., *Play, Dreams and Imitation in Childhood*, Norton, 1951

Storr, Anthony, *The Integrity of the Personality*, Pelican Book, Pelican, 1963

Wolff, Charlotte, *A psychology of Gesture*, Methuen, London, 1949

Art

Blunt, Anthony, *Picasso's Guernica*, Oxford University Press, London, 1969

Cinotti, Mia, *The Complete Paintings of Bosch*, Weidenfeld & Nicolson, London, 1969

Diehl, Gaston, *Max Ernst*, Crown Publishers Inc., New York, 1973

Fezzi, Elda, *Henry Moore*, Hamlyn 1972, Hamlyn House, Feltham, England

Holy, Ladislav, *Masks and Figures from Eastern & Southern Africa*, Paul Hamlyn, London, 1967

Klee, Paul, *Pedagogical Sketchbook*, Faber & Faber, London, first publ. 1925

Piggott, Juliet, *Japanese Mythology*, Hamlyn Publishing Group, London, 1969

Read, Herbert, *Education Through Art*,

Sorell, Walter, *The Duality of Vision*, Thames and Hudson, London, 1970

Trendall, A. D. & Webster, T. B. L., *Illustration of Greek Drama*, Phaidon, London, 1971

General

Bachelard, Gaston, *On Poetic Imagination and Reverie*, Bobbs-Merril Co., 1971

de Bono, Edward, *PO: Beyond Yes & No*, Penguin, England, 1972

Cooper, J. C., *Taoism, The Way of the Mystic*, The Aquarian Press, Wellingborough, Notts., 1972

Eliade, Mircea, *Rites and Symbols of Initiation*, Harper & Row, New York, 1958

Mann, Felix, *Acupuncture Cure of Many Diseases*, Heinemann Medical Books, London, 1971

Mc Luhan, M., *Understanding Media: The Extensions of Man*, McGraw-Hill, New York, 1964

Walker, Kenneth, *Diagnosis of Man*, Pelican Books, 1962

Walker, Kenneth, *A Study of Gurdjieff's Teaching*, Jonathan Cape, London, 1957

Wilhelm, R. (translator and editor), *The Secret of the Golden Flower, A Chinese Book of Life*, Routledge and Kegan Paul, London, 1931

Yu-Lan, Fung, *A Short History of Chinese Philosophy*, The Free Press, New York, 1948

176

Acknowledgements

We would like to express our thanks for encouragement and advice to John Allen, Elfriede and Julius Hollos, Hanna and Yehudah Paradise, Elijahu Ne'eman, Gerda Andrew, Moshe Feldenkrais, Gerda Geddes.

Many thanks to all our students for their interest, receptiveness and willingness to experiment; to our colleagues Yehudith Arnon, Alex Hadari, Molly Kenny, Jess Curtis and Iris Henson for their cooperation and understanding; to our friends Helen Chinoy and Anita Page from U.S.A. and to our many friends, too numerous to mention for reading the manuscript and contributing valuable advice.

We are greatly indebted to our photographers, mainly, Yehudah Paradise, and, Eliyahu Ne'eman, Claire McNamee, Terry Measham, Dov, Norman and Yoram as well as to Mary Irex, Ben Ami Traub, Tally Ne'eman and all our students.

For the permission to report on the Tate Gallery Project; to Macmillan Publishing Co., Inc. and Turnstone Books for the quotation by Richard Bach from Jonathan Livingstone Seagull; for permission to quote 4 lines from "A Prayer for Old Age" from THE COLLECTED POEMS OF W. B. YEATS of M. B. Yeats, Miss Anne Yeats, Macmillan London & Basingstoke and Macmillan Co. of Canada; to Denis Silk for the quotation from 'A Face A Stone'. To Editions Albin Michel Paris for the quotation from Romain Rolland.

To Noah Eshkol for permission to use the diagrams from Movement Notation by Noa Eshkol and Abraham Wachmann, published by the Movement Notation Society, Tel-Aviv.

Finally, many thanks are extended to the members and particularly the children of Kibbutz Yechiam, Western Galilee, where Nira Ne'eman developed most of her experience.

Notes on the Authors

Lea Bartal
Graduate of the Sigurd Leeder School for Modern Dance in London and the New Bezalel Art Academy in Jerusalem.
    Studied for many years in Israel with:
        Noa Eshkol
        Dr. Moshe Feldenkrais
        and recently in London
        the T'ai Chi Ch'uan with Mrs. G. Geddes
        Alexander Method with Katyah Michaeli.
    As secretary of the Movement Teachers Association in Israel organised and participated in many Seminars held in Israel with internationally known teachers such as Rosalia Chladek from Vienna, Gerda Alexander from Copenhagen, Annelise Widmann and Anna Sokolov from New York.
    Twenty years teaching took place in Israel in her own studio, at the Conservatory for Music in Jerusalem, with various Youth groups in Kibbutzim, New Immigrant settlements, Teachers Training College and various theatrical groups.
    In England: at Cardiff College of Music and Drama, East 15 Acting School, School of Theatre at Manchester Polytechnic where teaching full-time at present. During all those years choreographed for many festivals and celebrations with large groups of all ages, choreographing movement for plays with children and adults. Has also directed a number of plays with students in the Stables Theatre Manchester and worked with actors at Granada Television, and in the Prospect Theatre Company.

Nira Ne'eman
Graduate of Israel's Teacher's training College, specialising in movement and education through movement. She studied for many years with Israel's foremost teachers:
        Dr. Moshe Feldenkrais
        Gertrud Kraus
        Noa Eshkkl
        Ktyah Michaeli
        Yardenah Cohen
        and in London:
        at the Laban Institute of Movement,
        the Alexander Foundation, and

Tai Chi Ch'uan with Mrs. Gerda Geddes.

She has participated in many International Seminars held in Israel with teachers such as Rosalia Chladek from Vienna, Gerda Alexander from Copenhagen and others.

She taught for twenty years at Kibbutz Yechiam, Movement and modern educational dance; Dance Drama; Remedial Movement covering all age groups.

She is on the permanent staff of the Regional School of Dance and the Central Drama Studio in Western Galilee.

She has taught post graduate courses for teachers organised by the Ministry of Education and the Kibbutz Movement.

During these years she directed many festivals and celebrations, organised folk dancing, choreographed dances, staged movement for theatre and directed children's plays.

1971–1974 (sabbatical years): Work at the Tate Gallery (2 years) Guildford School of Acting, Dance and Drama Teachers; Courses for Teachers of Physical Education and Dance; Unicorn Theatre for Young Children (Guest Teacher).

She is now working in the School of Education, University of Haifa.